MARTIAL ARTS SERIES

Jujitsu
Techniques & Tactics

Doug Musser
3rd-Degree Black Belt — Dan Zan Ryu Jujitsu

Thomas A. Lang
4th-Degree Black Belt — Dan Zan Ryu Jujitsu
2nd-Degree Black Belt — Muso Shindo Ryu Iaido

Human Kinetics

Library of Congress Cataloging-in-Publication Data

Musser, Doug, 1951-
    Jujitsu : techniques & tactics / Doug Musser, Tom Lang.
      p. cm. -- (Martial arts series)
    Includes index.
    ISBN 0-88011-830-X
    1. Jiu-jitsu. I. Lang, Thomas A. (Thomas Allen) II. Title.
    III. Series.
    GV1114.M88 1999
    796.815'2--dc21
                                            99-19381
                                                CIP

ISBN: 0-88011-830-X

Chapter two is a revised edition of "The Roots of Jujitsu" in *An Introduction to Kodenkan Jujutsu,* published in 1979 by Thomas Lang.

Acquisitions Editor: Jeff Riley; **Developmental Editor:** Laura Hambly; **Assistant Editors:** Kim Thoren, Laura Majersky, Leigh LaHood, and Stephan Seyfert; **Copyeditor:** Anne M. Heiles; **Proofreader:** Bob Replinger; **Indexer:** Betty Frizzell; **Graphic Designer:** Robert Reuther; **Graphic Artist:** Tom Roberts; **Photo Editor:** Clark Brooks; **Cover Designer:** Jack Davis; **Photographer (cover):** Raymond Malace; **Photographer (interior):** Tom Roberts; **Printer:** United Graphics

Human Kinetics books are available at special discounts for bulk purchase. Special editions or book excerpts can also be created to specification. For details, contact the Special Sales Manager at Human Kinetics.

Printed in the United States of America   10 9 8 7 6 5 4 3 2

Human Kinetics
Web site: www.humankinetics.com

United States: Human Kinetics, P.O. Box 5076, Champaign, IL 61825-5076
800-747-4457
e-mail: humank@hkusa.com

Canada: Human Kinetics, 475 Devonshire Road, Unit 100, Windsor, ON N8Y 2L5
800-465-7301 (in Canada only)
e-mail: hkcan@mnsi.net

Europe: Human Kinetics, Units C2/C3 Wira Business Park, West Park Ring Road,
Leeds LS16 6EB, United Kingdom
+44 (0) 113 278 1708
e-mail: hk@hkeurope.com

Australia: Human Kinetics, 57A Price Avenue, Lower Mitcham, South Australia 5062
08 8277 1555
e-mail: liahka@senet.com.au

New Zealand: Human Kinetics, P.O. Box 105-231, Auckland Central
09-523-3462
e-mail: hkp@ihug.co.nz

THIS BOOK IS DEDICATED IN LOVING MEMORY TO PROFESSOR PATRICK BROWNE (1947–1996). DURING HIS LIFE, PROFESSOR BROWNE DEDICATED HIMSELF TO THE PRESERVATION AND PERPETUATION OF DAN ZAN RYU JUJITSU. HE WAS THE CONSUMMATE RENAISSANCE MAN, TEACHER, STUDENT, HEALER, WARRIOR, SCIENTIST, POET, OBSERVER, PUNDIT, AND STEADFAST FRIEND. TO ACCOMPANY PATRICK DOWN LIFE'S HIGHWAY, EVEN FOR A SHORT TIME, WAS ALWAYS ENRICHING, OFTEN ENTERTAINING, NEVER DULL, MOSTLY ENLIGHTENING, AND A RARE PRIVILEGE TO BE TREASURED. PATRICK NEVER HESITATED TO BE OF SERVICE TO HIS SENIORS, HIS CONTEMPORARIES, AND HIS STUDENTS. HE WAS A MAN OF REMARKABLE DEPTH AND BREADTH. HIS PASSING LEFT AN ENORMOUS VOID IN THE LIVES OF ALL WHOM HE TOUCHED, BOTH WITHIN AND OUTSIDE OF THE MARTIAL ARTS COMMUNITY. LIKE THE VIBRATIONS THAT RESULT FROM THE SINGLE, CRYSTALLINE TOLLING OF A GIANT BELL, HIS LESSONS CONTINUE TO TRAVEL OUTWARD, IMPACTING INDIVIDUALS FROM ALL WALKS OF LIFE. FOR BEING MY SENSEI AND MY FRIEND, I THANK YOU.

—DOUG MUSSER

CONTENTS

PREFACE

Y ou are about to be introduced to a very special Japanese martial art known as jujitsu. Developed over several hundred years of Japanese history, jujitsu has evolved and spread into various styles. Today, you can study styles of jujitsu that are broad-based and others that focus on specific types of skills. Some modern styles emphasize only grappling or throwing, or striking and kicking. Broad-based styles include aspects of these skills in addition to weapons use and defense, meditation, healing, and police tactics and techniques. Some styles are representative of truly classical jujitsu, retaining traditional philosophy and techniques, whereas others combine parts of several martial arts to accommodate the various demands of combat and interests of students in the 20th century. This book is based on a style of jujitsu that, along with its strong classical roots, has incorporated changes and adaptations to the modern world.

Jujitsu was born on the battlefield, where combat determined whether a technique was practical. Nevertheless, much of the art has been expanded and refined in the modern era—away from the battlefield. Studying true jujitsu is not accomplished in 10 easy lessons; its secrets have to be learned through long and diligent study. In addition, there is more to the study of jujitsu than meets the eye; it is more than physical technique.

This book is designed to help you look more deeply into what jujitsu can offer you and then decide whether you want what it has to offer. Use this book as a guide to help you clearly identify your purpose for wanting to learn jujitsu and the goals you hope to attain. Once you have done this, you can then set out to find a style, school, and instructor to meet your needs. To guide you in selecting a school or instructor, your reading here is designed to enable you to identify several key characteristics of solid styles and competent instructors.

For the experienced practitioner, this book will clarify the basics necessary to the practice of good jujitsu. It may identify aspects of jujitsu that you are unfamiliar with. If you practice a more eclectic style, it will help you see the roots from which modern day jujitsu has grown.

Although different styles vary in their scope, certain categories of technique are common to most of them. We illustrate these categories and give you an idea of how they can fit together into an overall curriculum. In addition, we give an overview of how competition is shaping the modern development of jujitsu. We also touch on subjects that are less commonly addressed in books on martial arts, such as traditional healing. However, the knowledge you gain from the practice of jujitsu is experiential in nature, and you must have an instructor, a *sensei*—the "one who has gone before"—to aid you in getting all you can from your efforts.

The organization of this book is not unlike the way many instructors introduce students to the various aspects of jujitsu itself. Chapter 1 begins by familiarizing you with the value of jujitsu and provides some criteria for selecting a good school. Chapter 2 sketches a brief history of jujitsu. Chapter 3 introduces you to the vocabulary, derived from its Japanese roots, used in most jujitsu schools and describes how a typical class is conducted.

In chapters 4 through 8 you get to the meat of jujitsu, the techniques. Fundamentals of falling, striking, throwing, grappling, submission techniques, and escapes and counters will be covered clearly and concisely. Chapter 9 shows how these aspects are combined to create effective jujitsu. Chapter 10 then addresses strategies and tactics for success in practice and combat. In chapter 11 you learn the various ways jujitsu can be practiced in a competitive form. Chapter 12 outlines the basics of conditioning and its importance to your study of jujitsu.

By reading this book you will gain a fair measure of what jujitsu has to offer you on several levels. All of us who have studied jujitsu more than a few years have had to unearth these understandings along the way. A book such as this one would have saved us a great deal of time and trouble. But knowing about the lessons you will learn and actually learning these lessons are two very different things. The latter requires a great deal of hard work and dedication. What we can share with you is that the rewards that come from such effort are more profound than you can possibly imagine. We wish you the best and believe that this book will help you along the way.

ACKNOWLEDGMENTS

I would first like to thank Professor Henry Okazaki for creating Dan Zan Ryu jujitsu. Professor Okazaki's lifelong dedication to the study of jujitsu, his tireless pursuit of the higher moral and ethical values that the study of jujitsu embodies, and his unbending intent on synthesizing a system of jujitsu that bridges (brilliantly I believe) the gap from this martial art's classical beginnings to its modern expression have ensured its future survival. His work has profoundly affected the lives of thousands of people. I remain ever mindful of an enormous debt of gratitude to you, my first teacher.

To the professors, sensei, and members of the American Judo and Jujitsu Federation (AJJF), I express my deepest appreciation for the many lessons and guidance you have shared with me throughout the years. To the many professors, sensei, and members of other Dan Zan Ryu organizations, I express my heartfelt gratitude for your kindness and many lessons. To all these professors, sensei, and members, thank you for your unflagging efforts in preserving and perpetuating this most profound system of Dan Zan Ryu jujitsu. *Ohana.*

To Sensei Gary Lescak, your entry into my life set me on a path of growth and enlightenment. Words cannot easily measure my profound gratitude for all your instruction and guidance. Thank you, my teacher and my friend. To Sensei Tom Hill, from the moment you first showed me the true meaning of *kokua,* you have continued to embody the highest ideals of jujitsu and have remained a true and constant friend. Thank you. To Sensei Raeford McIlwaine, thank you for being the warrior, brother, and friend that you are. I have the deepest respect for you. To Sensei Bob Thomas, this would not have been possible without you—thank you, my friend. To the sensei Maureen Browne, Mary Boland, Tim Boland, John Gussman, Ward Melenich, and Sohn Wechsler, the road we have traveled has been both difficult and painful. But the rewards have been many, not the least of which are your friendships. Thank you for everything. To Professors Tom Ball, Sig Kufferath, Ramon Ancho, Tom Jenkins, Jane Carr, Bob Hudson, and Don Cross, thank you for sharing your wisdom and experience. A special thank you to Sensei Bob Krull and Sensei Bob McKean for your many lessons and insights. To Sensei Tim Merrill, too, thank you for showing by your example what Professor Browne envisioned a sensei to be.

To my many jujitsu and restorative massage students, thank you for challenging me to become a sensei and for being constant reminders of why I love doing this.

To my loving wife, Jeri, without whose love, support, encouragement, and patience this book would never have been possible. Thank you so much.

To my parents, Bob and Helen, and the rest of my family, thank you for believing in me. To the students and sensei of the Martial Arts Training Service (MATS) in Aurora, Illinois, my deepest gratitude for the use of your dojo in photographing illustrations for this book.

A special thanks to Therese Egget, Jason Cartwright, Mike Poland, Dave Savell, Joe Tan, and Jane Tan for their help in shooting the photos for this book.

To my coauthor, Tom Lang, thank you for your guidance, contributions, and for steering me through this process of writing a book.

And to my student and steadfast friend, John Grimes—thanks for the critical eye.

—Doug Musser

CHAPTER

1

GETTING STARTED

he first question you must ask yourself is "What do I want from a martial art?" People study martial arts for a variety of reasons. Most hope to gain a means of self-defense. Others are looking for a way to stay in shape. Still others are drawn to the mystical and metaphysical aspects of martial arts. Many people have heard that martial arts help to develop self-discipline. There are a variety of reasons to study a martial art, and when you shop around for a martial art as a prospective student, you should have your purpose clearly in mind. This can go a long way toward helping you choose the martial art that is best for you.

There are many ways to classify martial arts. One of the most common considers whether an art is "hard" or "soft." Hard martial arts are characterized by linear striking, bone-to-bone blocking, and deflection of the opponent's attack to allow for powerful, rapid, and direct counterattack. Soft martial arts, on the other hand, are characterized by oblique and specialized striking, circular blocking and parrying, redirection of the opponent's attack to utilize its momentum, and painful submission and incapacitation techniques. More experienced martial artists say that hard and soft are not mutually exclusive, despite the fact that they are often taught that way. Examples of hard martial arts are karate, taekwondo, and Okinawan kenpo. Most people consider judo, aikido, and tai chi chuan softer styles of martial arts.

Jujitsu is usually classified as a relatively soft martial art. This is because one of the main principles of jujitsu is minimum expenditure of effort to achieve maximum result. Making use of this principle allows a person of smaller size the chance to beat a much larger opponent. Jujitsu takes advantage of the principles of leverage, balance, and momentum to utilize the opponent's own strength and force to defeat him.

Another way exists to classify martial arts, however: by their place of origin or where they come from. Jujitsu and aikido come from Japan. Taekwondo, hwrang do, and kuk sul won come from Korea. Tai chi chuan, pa kua, and choy li fut are examples of Chinese martial arts. Okinawan kenpo comes, of course, from Okinawa. Although this list is by no means exhaustive, it may convey the idea that it is useful to know the origin of the arts you are investigating.

And there are many other distinctions to consider. Is the particular martial art evolving or the same as it has always been? Does the art teach weapons (is a weapon the central focus)? Is the art taught in a traditional manner or, like many versions in the United States today, in a much more casual style? Of course, where you live also has some bearing on what is available to you, but only in the smallest of towns is the selection really limited. A search for available martial arts may begin with the Yellow Pages, where commercial schools are listed. But many good martial arts courses are also taught in local park districts, junior colleges, universities, and YMCAs or YWCAs.

VALUE OF JUJITSU

What does jujitsu have to offer? A martial art that comes from Japan, jujitsu was developed as part of the combat skills used by the samurai during the feudal era of Japanese history. Usually considered an unarmed form of fighting, it more accurately might be called a form of empty-hand combat that can make use of small weapons against either an armed or unarmed opponent.

Jujitsu is often regarded as a defensive art, yet in truth it employs both defensive and offensive tactics. The emphasis in most schools, however, is initially defensive. The jujitsu student develops skills in striking, kicking, throwing, joint-locking, choking, strangling, and grappling. In the beginning a student is taught basic skills in these areas with an emphasis on escaping from threatening situations. As a student's abilities increase, the emphasis turns to countering the attack and subduing the opponent. At still more advanced levels, the student works on combining all the skills to use them in both offensive and defensive situations.

This progression of skill acquisition may vary from school to school, of course, and from teacher to teacher. At some point the student may be introduced to the use of traditional smaller weapons and to knife and gun defenses. Depending on the style of jujitsu being taught, certain techniques may even be considered secret, part of the oral tradition only. That means they are not taught to everyone but to only the most serious and dedicated students; they are passed on from teacher to student only by oral instruction. Depending on the style, other more traditional arts may be taught—such as hog-tying or securing your opponent with ropes and wooden sticks. The more complete systems of jujitsu will also introduce students to healing and resuscitative arts as well as to meditation. Finally, many jujitsu systems will teach adjunct police tactics and techniques.

POLICE TACTICS

Police tactics and techniques are often part of the jujitsu curriculum. When the feudal era of Japan came to an end, the entire warrior caste was set adrift; many samurai turned to wandering and some turned to crime. The need for a capable police force was paramount, and the art they turned to was jujitsu. The flexibility of jujitsu lent itself to law enforcement's need for subduing and capturing criminals with a minimum of harm. It is the very fact that jujitsu has so many types of techniques that made it attractive and useful to the law enforcement of that era.

And to this day jujitsu is widely regarded as a martial art that gives law-enforcement officials many options for apprehending criminals. Not surprisingly, many jujitsu systems today teach police tactics and training and require senior students to develop courses of instruction for training law-enforcement officials.

The same aspects that make jujitsu useful for law enforcement appeal as well to many prospective students—that is, the wide variety of tools and techniques give you many options for dealing with an opponent. Most people are not interested in beating an attacker into submission but simply want to deflect the opponent's aggression. Where possible, subduing an opponent with a minimal amount of physical force is preferable.

Of course, some aggressors are bent and determined to cause a victim great harm. Well-trained jujitsu students can escalate their response; they have learned far more punishing and deadly techniques. In general, however, well-trained students avoid confrontation when possible and seek to defuse a deadly situation. If that is not possible, they are prepared to respond with whatever force is necessary.

Make no mistake, though: acquiring the level of skill necessary to have such flexible response takes a great deal of training. One of our teachers, Professor Patrick Browne, was fond of saying, "Jujitsu is not 10 easy lessons." And he was absolutely right. He also used to say, "You have to be tough to do jujitsu." That also is true. To practice and learn the many skills involved, you must have others to serve as the practice opponent.

This means many nights of being sore and tired are in store for any serious jujitsu student. That is why truly complete jujitsu systems teach healing and restorative arts—so that students may take care of each other and learn to cope with the inevitable small injuries that occur from training.

DEVELOPMENT OF MIND, BODY, DISCIPLINE, AND CHARACTER

Many martial arts are concerned with developing only a student's fighting skills. This is particularly true of the many eclectic variations of jujitsu one can now find, driven in part by the great popularity of Cage Matches, such as the Ultimate Fighting and Extreme Fighting contests, seen on television. Some people believe that to truly test a martial art's effectiveness, it must be done in combative venues. Nevertheless, what seems to be happening is that some of the best attributes of martial arts in general, and jujitsu in particular, are being ignored. These attributes—character development, self-discipline, and the development of mind-body coordination and awareness—are among the greatest benefits that training in jujitsu has to offer.

Character development comes from continually confronting one's limitations and shortcomings and finding ways to overcome them. Self-discipline comes from going to class day after day and practicing over and over again until you achieve progress. Mind-body awareness and coordination come from processing information first through the mind while being taught and then learning to translate this information into actual physical skills. Throughout this process you become ever more aware of your physical body and how to use it effectively.

Learning skills of proper breathing, balanced movement, and coordination of the entire body presents you with the challenge of integrating all these aspects to accomplish a goal. Jujitsu, because of the breadth of its techniques and skills, is uniquely suited to challenge students in every possible way. The skills you develop when confronted with so many challenges cause you to integrate new ways of learning and being that will carry over into your day-to-day life, off the mat.

CHOOSING A SCHOOL

When investigating jujitsu schools, recognize there are a variety of ways in which jujitsu schools are organized and run. The oldest styles of jujitsu in the United States are usually run on the more classical model of the traditional Japanese *dojo* (school). Respect for the teacher, style, and dojo are emphasized. The course of instruction is usually more formalized for the beginning student and only becomes more relaxed as the student gains in seniority and skill. More recent eclectic styles of jujitsu are not so formal in their presentation but are essentially tailored to appeal to students looking only for the acquisition of fighting skills. Be clear on what appeals to you most strongly when investigating jujitsu schools.

TEACHING STYLES

Instructors often follow a wide range of teaching styles. For instance in classical Japanese dojos, senior instructors often had little to do with beginning students, and left it to other senior students to bring the beginners along. This still exists in some styles taught in the United States. but more often it is simply a matter of expediency as teaching time is often limited. The *sensei* (school head) is responsible for teaching other senior students and may not have time to teach the beginners except occasionally. Still it seems best to avoid schools where the sensei has little to do with the beginners.

Upon investigating a school you should have the option to discuss your goals with the sensei, and good sensei make themselves available to do this. In a respectful manner it is OK to ask the sensei about his or her experience and background. Ask the sensei what the training goals are for both the students and the school. If the sensei is arrogant or distracted during this interview he or she is likely to be this way in the dojo. Interview some of the students as well. Ask them how they like the training and the school and ask them if their needs and goals are being met. Ask within your community about the reputation of the school and the instructor. If the reputation is poor or the answers avoid the question, you might want to consider another school. Good schools and sensei will freely talk about their training and experiences but will do so in a humble manner. They may also talk about other schools and styles in the area but should do so in a respectful manner. Putting down other schools and styles is usually a sign that true humility is lacking. Good schools and sensei will ask you to observe a class and may even offer you a chance to participate on a limited basis. A good sensei wants only good and seriously interested students, so recognize that you are probably being assessed as well.

ASSESSING THE SCHOOL

Again, check the format of the school and look for some key indicators. Are the students respectful of the sensei and each other? Are the students paying attention to their lessons and are they concentrating on their practice? If the students are goofing around, engaged in horseplay, or are talking and joking around a

In this jujitsu class the sensei works directly with the students.

lot, this is a bad sign. Whatever format the school employs, whether classical or relaxed, there should be no question as to who is in charge. A typical training regimen in a jujitsu dojo includes good warm-up and stretching, practice of rolls and falls, training skills such as falling and throwing, joint locks, grappling, and striking and blocking. Other skill training is appropriate according to skill level. Some time is usually allotted for cool-down, massage, or meditation. A typical class should last about two hours. A student should be able to attend class at least twice per week, but three or more times is better. Even once per week, if the student is serious, attentive, and consistent, will allow for progress, but the progress will be slow. But three times per week really seems to make for a much higher learning curve. Many senior students will make themselves available for additional training if circumstances allow. Remember, a dedicated and serious student is a delight to any sensei and a great addition to any school.

Once you've assessed the school and the sensei, take some time to reconsider your personal goals. In fact you should have told the sensei in the interview what your goals are and how you think they can be met. The sensei will probably explain to you that

ᒣYPICAL DOJO RULES

- Arrive on time.
- Dress appropriately.
- Show respect for instructors and other students.
- Understand and remember the customs of bowing.
- Pay attention.
- Do not roughhouse or play around.
- Avoid unnecessary talking.
- When appropriate, ask questions but do so respectfully.
- Do not attempt techniques that have not been taught to you.
- Report all injuries to the instructor.
- Keep finger and toenails trimmed.
- Alcohol and drugs are forbidden.

indeed they can be met but perhaps not in the way you envision. That is OK though. A good sensei recognizes that students will come to him or her for many reasons and will seek to explain how a person's goals may be achieved. Remember, a good sensei, once accepting you as a student, will do his or her best to train you but will retain the freedom to see it through as he or she deems best.

DOJO PROTOCOL

Protocols will vary from dojo to dojo according to the style and the sensei. Traditional type dojos may have a rigid set of rules and behaviors required of the students, while contemporary dojos may have a more relaxed set of guidelines to govern student behaviors. Above is a sample of typical rules a student is likely to find in most dojos.

EQUIPMENT

Equipment requirements will vary according to school and style. In most dojos the most important piece of equipment is the *gi* (uniform). Most equipment catalogs refer to this uniform as the judo gi. It consists of a jacket, drawstring pants, and an *obi* (belt) and differs from the traditional karate gi by being made of a heavier weight of cotton and is reinforced with a great deal of stitching. The judo gi usually comes in single- and double-weight versions. Single weight is more than adequate for those starting out and it is less costly. However, serious students usually acquire a double-weight gi because they tend to last longer. Another variation used by some dojos is a gi made of a heavy duck cloth cotton that lacks the extensive extra stitching. Gi's come in a variety of colors, some of which may be required by a given dojo, but most jujitsu schools use a basic white or off-white color, reserving other colors, if any, for instructors. At advanced levels, other equipment needs will most likely include practice weapons. Among these will be *tanto* (knife), *tanju* (hand gun), *bokken* (wooden practice sword), *jo* (short staff), and *bo* (long staff). These can be acquired through martial arts supply stores or by mail order. The student will find that a sound equipment bag is necessary at some point to carry the gi and practice weapons. In addition, many students will find a notebook is necessary to record what they learn, and as time goes by students usually begin to carry various balms, liniments, athletic tape and underwrap, water bottle, towel, band-aids, and nail clippers.

RANKING SYSTEM

Most dojos utilize the kyu-dan ranking system developed by Professor Jigoro Kano for judo. Kyu ranks begin with white belt (which comes with the uniform at purchase) and progress from higher numbers to lower ones through different colors (see table 1.1). Each rank level will have a series of requirements that the student must meet and be tested on. Within each school, rank requirements are set and adhered to, but they are likely to vary from school to school and rarely are the same for different styles. When the student has acquired all skills necessary at ikkyu (first kyu), they may test for shodan (first black). Dan ranks reverse the number progression, starting with 1 and going through 10 (jodan). The reversing of the number progression at the dan level symbolizes that the student is starting to learn all over again but in a different manner. That is to say that progression through the kyu ranks allows the student to acquire the basic physical skills necessary to do jujitsu as well as an understanding of the appro-

TABLE 1.1
Kyu-Dan Ranking

Name	Level	Belt
Rokyu	6th kyu	white
Gokyu	5th kyu	blue
Yonkyu	4th kyu	green
Sankyu	3rd kyu	brown
Nikkyu	2nd kyu	brown
Ikkyu	1st kyu	brown
Shodan	1st dan	black
Nidan	2nd dan	black
Sandan	3rd dan	black
Yondan	4th dan	black
Godan	5th dan	black
Rokkudan	6th dan	black or red and white
Shichidan	7th dan	black or red and white
Hachidan	8th dan	black or red and white
Kudan	9th dan	black or red and white
Judan	10th dan	black, red and white, or solid red

Colors in the kyu ranks may vary according to style; they may actually start at the 10th level (jukyu). Notice also the color variations present in the dan ranks. This variation is school- or style-specific.

priate attitudes that govern the application of the skills and techniques. At the dan level the student is introduced to more difficult skills, more lethal techniques, and more esoteric aspects of jujitsu. This in effect requires the student to start over in how he or she synthesizes the art, thus beginning at 1 and progressing upward through 10. In most jujitsu systems, all the techniques are taught by fourth or fifth dan level, and rank progression is subsequently based upon service to the style and time in grade. While more senior students begin to teach other students in the kyu ranks, passage to the dan level implies assumption of the responsibilities of sensei. Sensei are responsible for a great deal more than teaching technique.

The student should remember that ranking is a relative method of distinguishing skill levels and serves as a means by which the student and instructor can gauge progress. However, the student should strive to cultivate humility and remember that the purpose of the belt, regardless of the color, is to keep the jacket closed.

Once you decide to go with a particular style or school, you will have a role to fill as a good student. Good students, upon arriving at the school, will learn to leave their personal problems at the door so that they may fully concentrate on their instruction. Good students are prepared to take instruction as it is given and do their best. Good students have respect for their sensei, their seniors, and the other students. Good students work hard to understand what humility is all about and in so doing will be able to carry it over to the rest of their lives. Good students learn, grow, and gradually achieve a whole new level of awareness about everything.

Good luck to you on finding the best jujitsu school available. By studying jujitsu you will open doors in your life that you never imagined were there, and the benefits will last throughout your entire life!

CHAPTER

2

ROOTS
OF JUJITSU*

ujitsu is a traditional Japanese form of unarmed combat. The correct transliteration is *jujutsu*, although *jujitsu* and *jiu-jitsu* (in British English) are commonly accepted spellings. We use jujitsu throughout this book because it is the most familiar spelling. *Ju* means "pliability," "flexibility," or "to give way." *Jitsu* means a fighting form or practice (as opposed to a *do,* which is a more spiritual form of martial training). Jujitsu, then, means "the martial practice of giving way" or, more broadly, "the practice of giving way without giving up or giving in."

Contrary to popular belief, jujitsu does not mean "the gentle art." Many of its techniques are far from gentle, although deceptively little strength may be needed to perform them. Strength is a factor in most techniques, but it must be applied according to the principle of *seiryoku-zenyo*: the most efficient use

*The original version of this chapter appeared as "A Brief History of Jujitsu," in Tom Lang's, *An Introduction to Kodenkan Jujutsu* (1979, published privately as a text for beginning jujitsu students at California State University, Chico).

of energy. One jujitsu master, Iso Mataemon, describes jujitsu this way:

> The use of power in *jujutsu* is greatly necessary. But it is only when such power is not used in excess that it stands the test of the principle of *ju*. Another aspect of the use of power must be born in mind, too. From the early stages of a trainee's development in *jujutsu*, he must always be careful to avoid reliance on physical strength, for such is an obstacle in the way of his progress toward the gaining of skill in technique. After the trainee has developed a creditable technique, however, then the use of power is acceptable and, in fact, absolutely necessary to his effectiveness in dealing with an adversary. *Jujutsu* is "pliant" and "flexible" in this way. (Draeger 1973, p. 122)

Jujitsu can be both offensive and defensive—again, contrary to popular belief. Although martial philosophies usually stress restraint, they also recognize that attack or "seizing the initiative" may at times be appropriate, and jujitsu is suitable for these occasions.

THE HISTORY OF JUJITSU

Japanese history can be divided into eight periods:

- The Ancient period, before 650 A.D.
- The Nara period, from 650 to 793 A.D.
- The Heian period, from 794 to 1191 A.D.
- The Kamakura period, from 1192 to 1336 A.D.
- The Muromachi or Ashikaga period, from 1337 to 1563 A.D.
- The Azuchi or Momoyama period, from 1564 to 1602 A.D.
- The Edo or Tokugawa period, from 1603 to 1867 A.D.
- The Modern or Meiji period, from 1868 to the present.

The first account of jujitsu-like tactics in Japan dates to the Ancient period. In the *Kojiki* (Record of Ancient Matters), a historical writing, there is an account of Nomino-Sukune wrestling with and finally kicking to death Tajima-no-Kehaya. This battle, which took place in 23 B.C., is usually credited with being the origin of *sumai*, a combat form of *sumo* wrestling that developed into several empty-hand styles of combat, *jujitsu* among them.

During the Nara period, sumai and sumo were supported by the imperial family. These forms developed further in the Heian period and began to be used in conjunction with weapons, primarily the bow, spear, and sword. *Atemi*, the art of striking vital points of the body, was practiced with the butt ends of these weapons in close-quarter fighting. These techniques became a part of what would eventually be called jujitsu. *Daito Ryu* Jujitsu (or *Aikijujitsu*), a martial tradition (or *ryu*) that emerged during the later part of this period is the foundation on which modern *aikido* is based.

During the Kamakura period, Japan's feudal era, the military class (or *bushi*) accelerated the development of grappling techniques, which are an important part of jujitsu. These techniques, used when the major weapon was lost, involved close-quarter fighting, especially with knives or short swords. *Yoroi kumi-uchi* was a form of grappling used against an opponent wearing full armor. Although these techniques were developed for armored combatants, the principles were readily transferable to unarmed and unarmored combat.

The *Tenshin Shoden Katori Shinto Ryu* was founded in the 1400s during the Muromachi period, making this tradition one of the oldest (and most influential) martial systems in Japan. It contained a form of grappling called *yawara-ge* ("peacemaker") that could be used independently of weapons, although it usually involved weapons such as the *kodachi* (a short sword) and was not preferred to the use of major weapons. Miyamoto Musashi, Japan's great swordsman, studied yawara-ge, to which he attributed his great skill in *kakushi-jitsu*, the art of using small, concealable weapons. Another martial system, the *Muso-Jikiden Ryu*, included 100 techniques for fighting in armor that were collectively called *yawara-gi* ("meekness"). Again, these techniques could be applied with or without a weapon. All of these arts contributed to what we today call jujitsu.

THE DEVELOPMENT OF JUJITSU
IN UNARMED COMBAT

From 1467 until 1574, primarily during the Muromachi period, continual civil wars stimulated the development of all military arts. The techniques that would later become jujitsu were still secondary to the use of weapons, although they continued to augment the close-quarter use of weapons. For example, the *Takenouchi Ryu* (or *Takeuchi Ryu*), founded in 1532, included in-fighting techniques against an opponent clad in the light armor of gauntlets and leggings. These jujitsu-like techniques were called *kogu soku* or *koshi no mawari* (literally, "around the hips").

The Azuchi or Momoyama period was relatively peaceful. Presumably, empty-hand techniques continued to be developed. The term *kumi-uchi* eventually became the term for all the empty-hand arts of the period.

The Edo or Tokugawa period was an important time for jujitsu. Commoners were prohibited from carrying weapons, so they turned to empty-hand forms of combat. During this period, the term *jujitsu* became associated with these forms and replaced the term *kumi-uchi* in general use. But commoners lacked the martial experience—the expertise with weapons from which the unarmed arts developed—and the instruction necessary to create combat-ively sound systems. These common forms of "jujitsu," such as they were, soon became the practice of criminals and of the *nanushi,* the "bouncers" in houses of prostitution. The *bushi* (or soldiers) continued to practice their fighting forms, but these were kept secret within the ryu, which was often restricted to family or clan members. Some schools of jujitsu also became more aesthetic during this time: they began to develop the *practice* of the art as a value in its own right, as a form of philosophical and spiritual discipline, as well as preparation for combat.

Jujitsu was also simply called *yawara* during the Edo period. In the late 1600s, the *Sekiguchi Ryu* included a style of yawara based on sumo and suitable for use with weapons. The *Oguri Ryu*, founded in 1616, included techniques called *wajitsu* (the art of softness). These techniques were modified from those of *yoroi kumi-uchi* to be used against opponents wearing the street clothes of the Edo period. The *Nagao Ryu* included what it called *taijitsu* (body arts), a general term for empty-hand techniques that be-came popular among commoners in the period. This ryu was also noted for its kakushi-jitsu techniques.

THE DEVELOPMENT OF JUJITSU AS A PHILOSOPHICAL DISCIPLINE

Kito Ryu jujitsu was founded during the Edo period. This ryu, a system of combat-effective techniques, both armed and unarmed, is the foundation for much of *Kodokan Judo*, including modern sport judo. Eventually, the techniques became aesthetically oriented. Terada Kan'emon, the fifth headmaster of Kito Ryu, founded *Jikishin Ryu* jujitsu after he retired from the Kito Ryu. He is credited with the first use of the word *judo* and with establishing the practice of empty-hand techniques as a discipline with philosophical implications.

In the early 1800s, Iso Mataemon founded the *Tenjin Shin'yo Ryu*. This ryu was completely devoted to jujitsu and emphasized atemi (strikes) and *kata* (form) in mastering the aesthetic and combat applications of jujitsu. From this time on, many martial arts also began to incorporate the concepts of Zen Buddhism into their teachings, thus formalizing the practice of the art as a philosophical discipline directed toward the Zen concept of enlightenment. Thus, *kyujitsu* (archery) began to include the practice of *kyudo*, an art devoted entirely to the discipline of drawing the bow and releasing the arrow, not necessarily to accurately placing arrows in a target. (In kyudo, the arrow is usually released into a target only two meters away.) So, too, did *kenjitsu* (swordfighting) begin to include *kendo* (fencing with bamboo staves, now a competitive sport), and *iaijitsu* (drawing and cutting with the sword in indoor and urban settings) begin to include *iaido* (the art of sword drawing for form and technique). In contrast to the strictly martial orientation of the "jitsu" traditions, the "do" disciplines added a strong focus on *how the art was practiced*, in addition to (and sometimes instead of) the martial applications.

The golden age of jujitsu lasted from the late 1600s to the mid-1800s. After this time the combat-effective forms of jujitsu rapidly disintegrated. Still, during this period, 725 different martial ryu included techniques that might be called jujitsu.

In 1882, shortly after the beginning of the Meiji period, Jigoro Kano founded Kodokan Judo. Professor Kano studied many of the old jujitsu schools and became proficient in the *Kito Ryu* and *Tenjin Shin'yo Ryu*. Jujitsu was still associated with criminals and cheap exhibitions of fighting "skill." Professor Kano was principal of the Tokyo Higher Normal School and the first president of the Japan Society of Physical Education (an organization similar to the Amateur Athletic Association in the United States), in addition to being a jujitsu master. He made jujitsu a respectable form of physical education that was eventually taught in public schools throughout the country. He eliminated the obviously dangerous techniques, modified others so that they could be practiced safely, and developed a curriculum for teaching the techniques that resulted in what is called *Kodokan Judo*. Although he is remembered more for his development of sport judo, he also preserved many of the older jujitsu techniques. These techniques are still taught to higher-ranking students. He also established the ranking system used by many martial arts today, that of the *kyu-dan* (class-grade) system of 10 *kyu* or student ranks, which are generally indicated by colored belts or by colored tabs on belts, and 10 *dan* or black-belt instructor ranks, which are usually distinguished by different markings on a black or a red belt.

Professor Kano adopted three ways to practice his system. First was *kata* (literally, "dance") or prearranged techniques to be practiced unhurriedly, smoothly, and gracefully to develop skill and coordination. Second was *randori* (free play), a more rigorous form of practice in which two partners helped each other to learn in a friendly exchange of throws, holds, chokes, and joint-locks. Third was *shiai* ("battle") or competition with rules. It is said that *kata* trains the body; randori trains the mind; and shiai trains the spirit.

Judo as we know it today has become highly competitive. This emphasis on competition was probably not Professor Kano's intent, but Western influences after World War II, including the inclusion of judo in the Olympic Games in 1964, have made shiai the focus of training in many judo schools.

THE GROWTH OF JUJITSU
IN THE UNITED STATES

With the reopening of Japan to the Western world in the 1800s and the onset of the Meiji Restoration, the entire political structure of Japan changed, and for the first time westerners gained access to many aspects of Japanese culture. Practitioners of many of the Japanese arts began to travel the world demonstrating their skills. Jujitsu practitioners traveled to Europe, the United States, and South America giving exhibitions and challenging famous wrestlers and boxers to public matches. President Theodore Roosevelt was so impressed with jujitsu that he began to take

lessons in the White House. Law enforcement and military officials quickly recognized the effectiveness of jujitsu as a means of
subduing criminals. Dozens of small instruction manuals were
printed in the United States in the early 1900s, touting the virtues
of jujitsu as means of personal self-defense. It was with the
beginning of World War II, however, that jujitsu began to become
popular in the United States.

During the war in the Pacific, Allied forces often engaged
Japanese ground troops in hand-to-hand combat. Rather rapidly,
jujitsu techniques began to appear in hand-to-hand combat courses
and in unarmed combat field manuals of that time. Many servicemen developed an interest in learning not only the techniques of
jujitsu but also the philosophies and moral tenets that had become
part of many jujitsu traditions.

One such system, *Dan Zan Ryu* ("cedar mountain" or "island"
system, after the Hawaiian Islands where it was taught), illustrates this phenomenon. Compiled by Professor Henry S. Okazaki
in the 1920s and 1930s, it is a synthesis of several of the classical
jujitsu systems. Crediting the practice of jujitsu with helping him
to recover from a serious attack of tuberculosis, Professor Okazaki
dedicated his life to the study of the martial arts. Learning all that
he could of jujitsu in the Hawaiian Islands, he later traveled to
Japan and gained access to other classical systems, as well as to
Kodokan Judo. Nor did he limit his studies to jujitsu; he also
studied sumo, Western wrestling, Western boxing, Chinese boxing (*kung fu*), Filipino knife fighting (today usually referred to as
the arts of *kali*, *escrima*, or *arnis de mano*), Hawaiian *lua* (a form
of unarmed combat native to Hawaii), and Okinawan karate. (In
fact, the first karate class taught in the United States and its
territories was held in Professor Okazaki's jujitsu school.) He is
said to have chosen the name *Dan Zan Ryu* to honor his kung fu
teacher, who loved the Hawaiian Islands. He named his *dojo*
(school) the *Kodenkan* (in the expanded translation, The School
for the Transmission of Esoteric Zen Teachings), and there he
sought to preserve classical jujitsu techniques as well as the
practice of martial arts as a spiritual discipline.

Although the Kodenkan was in the territory of Hawaii, it was
initially closed to Westerners. This restriction was consistent
with the prevailing Japanese attitude of the time, which was to
limit access to the arts and not to teach foreigners. The notable

This tokonoma features pictures of Professor Henry Okazaki (right) and Professor Patrick Browne.

exception to this was Professor Kano and his Kodokan Judo system.

Professor Okazaki was a skilled masseur and healer—in addition to teaching jujitsu, he made his living as a physical therapist—who learned traditional healing and restorative arts as part of his study of jujitsu and other martial arts. It was through the advice and persuasion of a Swedish masseur with whom he studied that he eventually opened his school to westerners. From the 1930s until the 1950s, thousands of American servicemen, among others, were trained in *Dan Zan Ryu* jujitsu and carried their knowledge back to the mainland. Today, several organizations carry on Professor Okazaki's teachings across the United States. Some of these more traditional-styled organizations may even have tokonomas, or shrines, (as pictured above) that honor founding fathers like Professor Okazaki.

Many other styles of jujitsu are taught in the United Stated today, such as *Hakko Ryu* jujitsu, *Juko Ryu* jujitsu, *Miyama Ryu* jujitsu, and the more recent import from Brazil, *Gracie* jujitsu, to name but a few. Some of these styles have traditional roots; others are modern hybrids, compiled since World War II. In addition, several martial arts from other countries also use jujitsu-like techniques, such as Korean *hapkido*, Russian *sambo*, Chinese *chin-na*, Filipino *kali*, and, of course, western wrestling.

In a real sense, jujitsu is timeless. Its future depends not on how it evolves but on how its practitioners evolve. Jujitsu can be a superior form of physical culture, a challenging competitive sport, and an effective fighting art. That is, jujitsu practitioners now have the options of training as stylists, competitors, or fighters—or some combination of these perspectives. Each has its advantages and disadvantages; the secret is to know what you want from the art and to study with someone who approaches the art from that perspective.

CHAPTER

3

LANGUAGE AND CUSTOMS OF JUJITSU

n many jujitsu classes, commands and techniques are usually given in Japanese. Several of the more contemporary styles, however, use mostly English terms, which may or may not be translations of the Japanese. In practice, you are most likely to encounter some mixture of Japanese and English terms. This mixture is often useful in teaching English-speaking students and should not be interpreted as disrespect for the art or for the country of its origin.

A good example is the term *dojo*. A dojo is a school or place of study. Historically, a dojo was a permanent training hall, but today a jujitsu class might be taught in a wrestling room at a university, in a recreation room of a municipal park, or in a gymnasium at a YMCA or YWCA. Consequently, many students and instructors refer to their workout space as their dojo, even if their jujitsu class follows an aerobics workout and comes just before a gymnastics class. The English terms are usually self-explanatory, however, so this chapter is designed primarily to familiarize you with those Japanese terms you are most likely to encounter in your studies. Beyond that, we explain some concepts unique to the martial arts that have no English equivalents.

LANGUAGE DIFFERENCES

Many Japanese martial arts use the same terms, although some may have unique terms—and some common terms have different meanings. There are many reasons for this similarity in terminology. One is the language itself. Written English is phonetic; letters represent the sounds for the spoken terms. In contrast, however, Japanese characters are generally *pictographic* (the character is literally a picture of the thing it represents) or *ideographic* (the character combines two or more pictographs to suggest a concept or idea). Often the characters each have more than one meaning, so you may need to know how the word is used to determine which meaning is intended.

Two styles might also have the same name for two different mechanical actions. For example, in one style, *ude tori* ("arm break") may refer to a technique in which the elbow is attacked with a forearm, whereas in the other, the arm may be broken over the shoulder. You can see that although the techniques differ, they are each applied to the arm. The opposite may be true as well; two styles may have different names for the same technique. For example, both *ukemi* and *sutemi* refer to techniques for landing safely after being thrown. Ukemi means to fall. Sutemi, however, means "to throw oneself down." The difference in emphasis is clear and important: if you adopt the attitude of ukemi, you have accepted that you have been thrown and are waiting to fall safely. If you adopt the attitude of sutemi, you accept that you are being thrown, but rather than wait to fall, you throw yourself down. You take the throw away from your opponent and instead use the momentum of the throw as part of a counter. In other words, you give way without giving up or giving in.

MASTERING THE TERMINOLOGY

Listed below are some of the most common terms you are likely to encounter in a jujitsu school. Pronunciation guidelines are included to help you learn the correct Japanese pronunciation.

GENERAL TERMS

Japanese	English
dojo (doh-jo)	a school or training hall
sensei (sen-say)	a head instructor; teacher
tatami (ta-ta-me)	a six-foot by three-foot mat, traditionally made of woven grass and rice straw, that covers the floor of the dojo.
ryu (roo)	a style or tradition, here, of martial arts
goshinjitsu (go-shin-jit-soo)	self-defense
kyu (que)	a colored belt rank
dan (don)	a black belt rank

TRAINING TERMS

Japanese	English
seiza (say-za)	kneeling; the position in which you sit on your heels
kata (kah-tah)	form; in jujitsu, a single technique or several techniques in a sequence
kaiten (kai-ten)	wheel; rolls
sutemi (soo-tem-ee)	a fall, but implies "to abandon oneself or body"
ukemi (oo-kem-ee)	a fall
nage (nah-gay)	a throw
uke (oo-key)	the attacker; the one on whom the technique is executed

tori (tor-ee)	the defender, the one who executes the technique; also a hold on part of the body
kake (ka-key)	the execution of a technique
keri (care-ee)	a kick
atemi (ah-tay-me)	striking, refers to striking a particular target for a particular effect
hazushi (ha-zoo-she)	escape
katate (ka-ta-tay)	single hand
ryote (rye-oh-tay)	double hand
morote (more-oh-tay)	two-hand(ed)
harai (har-eye)	sweep
gari (gar-ee)	reap
gama (gah-ma)	sickle
hane (hah-ney)	springing
tsukikomi (su-key-comb-ee)	thrusting
garami (gar-ahm-ee)	joint lock
gaeshi (ga-ae-shee)	overturn
tomoe (toe-moi)	circle
otoshi (oh-toe-shee)	downward (in jujitsu it usually means drop)
kuzushi (coo-zoo-shee)	off-balancing
tsukuri (sue-coo-ree)	fitting in
shime or jime (she-may)	constriction, often as in a choke or a strangle but referring to constriction of other body parts as well
gatame (gah-tom-ee)	hold-down
katsu (cot-sue)	resuscitation technique
gyaku (gyah-coo)	reverse
tanto (tawn-toe)	knife
shuto (shoo-toe)	knife's edge
daito (die-toe)	sword

katana (ka-ta-na)	specific type of sword
tanju (tawn-jew)	gun
bo (bo)	staff
hanbo (hawn-bo)	half-staff

DIRECTIONAL TERMS

Japanese	English
kiotsuke (ki-oat-ski)	attention
shomen (show-mehn)	front
rei (ray)	bow
hajime (ha-ja-may)	begin
yame (yah-may)	stop
matte (mah-tay)	wait, although often used to mean stop
ushiro (u-she-row)	rear
yoko (yo-ko)	sideward
hibara (he-bar-ah)	side
mae (my)	forward
mawashi (mah-wa-she)	round
jodan (joe-dawn)	upper
gedan (gay-dawn)	lower

PARTS OF THE BODY

Japanese	English
dho (doe)	body
kubi (coo-be)	neck
mune (moo-nay)	chest
ude (oo-day)	arm
kote (ko-tay)	forearm, also refers to piece of armor covering the forearm
empai (em-pie) or hiji (he-gee)	elbow
tekubi (tay-koo-be)	wrist

te (tay)	hand
yubi (you-be)	finger or fingers
goshi (go-she) or koshi (ko-she)	hip or loin
kin (kin)	testicle
momo (moh-moh)	thigh
hiza (he-za)	knee
ashi (ah-she)	leg or foot, sometimes ankle

This glossary is by no means exhaustive. You are likely to encounter many more terms in your training. Realize, too, that when some of these terms are combined, the meanings may not follow a direct translation of the definitions we have listed.

Some of the more colorful terms to describe a technique may be used to convey a particular feel of that technique (as opposed to a straightforward description). For instance, a technique named *arashi otoshi* could be translated as "storm drop"; this tells you little about how the technique is configured, but it certainly conveys the spirit of the technique and the effect one hopes to achieve with it. The same might be said of a technique named *tora nage*, which means "tiger throw." Contrast this with a technique called *katate hazushi*, which means "single-hand escape": the term gives you a much clearer idea of what the technique comprises but still does not spell out how it is to be done. The reason is that there are literally dozens of ways to execute this technique. However, in many styles of jujitsu there is usually a standard form, or *kata,* that a student is taught; the other ways of executing it then are termed variations.

In one jujitsu style a technique may be called *ude shigarami,* while in another style the same technique is called *kote shigarami.* The first translates to "arm, arm capture," whereas the second translates to "forearm, arm capture." The literal translations are redundant, yet they both define an arm capture. A more contemporary style is likely to refer more simply to any arm capture as a *shigarami.*

So you can see that without the English translations of techniques, the practice of jujitsu could be confusing. But during the early phase of training most jujitsu instructors will keep the terminology fairly simple and provide students with a list of translations or English equivalent descriptions. As you progress through your training, these terms will become much more familiar.

A TYPICAL PRACTICE

By now you probably understand that there is a great deal of variation in styles and approaches to teaching jujitsu. We turn to explaining how a typical practice might be conducted in a style that upholds classical traditions. Remember, however, that the sensei may conduct a class in any manner he or she wishes. A good example of an atypical class might be one about police tactics, taught in a parking lot in street clothes.

STARTING CLASS

A typical practice will begin with a call to line up. Students line up according to seniority, the most senior member on the right, as they face the sensei. If the class is a regular, day-to-day practice, the bow is executed standing. If the class is a more formal one, the students and sensei begin in the *seiza* (kneeling position). The command *"Kiotsuke"* (attention) is given. This is followed by *"Shomen ni, rei"* (both students and sensei face the front wall, where pictures of the founder and flags perhaps are placed, and bow). Then the command *"Sensei ni, rei"* is given, and the sensei turns to face the students; both students and sensei bow to each other.

The bow, as in all things Japanese, can hold a world of information. Suffice it to say that in jujitsu it is a sign of mutual respect. Throughout a class, a student will often bow to an instructor as a show of respect for the immediate instruction just received. Students working out with each other will also bow to each other to signal their mutual respect as well, and to signal that they are ready to begin and end their activity. Furthermore, all students bow into and out of the dojo whenever entering or leaving. This bow shows respect, and it also is a symbolic gesture that participants leave the outside world behind when they enter, so as not to be distracted—and they assume it again when they leave.

JUJITSU WORKOUT

Once the class is bowed in, the sensei may direct the senior student to conduct conditioning and stretching exercises for the entire class. The sensei may choose to participate or observe. Stretching is fundamental to jujitsu practice. One definition of jujitsu is "the flexible art." To be flexible in mind and body is absolutely necessary in jujitsu. During the course of a class, the student's body is put through a wide range of positions and constrictions; flexibility helps prevent injury.

Next the students are led through *kaiten* and *sutemi*, or rolls and falls. Before students can learn to throw other people, they must first learn to take falls. *Nage* (throwing) is central to all that is practiced in jujitsu. In kaiten and sutemi, students learn the value of remaining relaxed. And, indeed, relaxation is fundamental to being able to act and react without hesitation.

Once finished with these preliminary exercises, a sensei may break the class down into groups according to skill levels. Beginners usually concentrate on learning kaiten, sutemi, yawara, and basic nage. More experienced students may practice *shime,* grappling and ground fighting, as well as basic striking and blocking. More advanced students will often concentrate their practice on combining all their basic skills together, working on timing, flow, and transition.

Because flexibility is key to everything in jujitsu, it follows that the sensei may be very flexible in how he or she may conduct the practice. The sensei may periodically regroup all the students to teach them a very fundamental principle, then let them practice applying the principle according to the individual students' skills and knowledge. At some point the class may engage in *randori* (competition throwing). Or perhaps competitive ground fighting is offered, affording the chance for engaging in some free play. To ensure the students' safety, rules apply in both randori and ground fighting, observed under the watchful eye of the sensei or senior student. For instance, no striking is allowed in randori; in ground fighting, submission techniques are applied but with control. Both of these rules allow the student to practice application of the kata techniques. Black belts or *dan* ranks usually practice in closed sessions alone with the sensei. Finally, *goshin jitsu* (self-defense) is practiced.

ENDING CLASS

Classes often wind down with the sensei teaching massage or healing techniques. This allows students to ease the various aches and pains acquired from vigorous training. Good jujitsu sensei are well schooled in a wide variety of traditional and modern healing arts in order to care for their students.

TRAINING SCHEDULE

In the classical jujitsu dojo, classes were conducted daily—and sometimes twice a day. Serious students were expected to attend all classes. It has long been a tradition in jujitsu that senior students teach the more junior ones, so the many classes afforded students the opportunity to teach others. The benefits and rewards one gets from teaching others cannot be easily measured. Teaching is an essential part of jujitsu training, and all students are being groomed to become competent and effective teachers. Contemporary schools, however, usually conduct only three to four classes per week, so class content at any given time may vary from what we have outlined here. Ultimately, however, all these aspects plus many others are included in the overall curriculum of a good jujitsu school.

You now have an idea of the vocabulary you will encounter in most jujitsu classes. Although the Japanese terms for techniques are often confusing to students during the learning stage, understanding how the terms are constructed and what they refer to can facilitate your using and remembering them. And now that you understand the fundamental protocols of a class, you won't feel you've stepped into a different dimension. It's time now to look more specifically at what you'll be learning.

CHAPTER

4

FALLS AND ROLLS

Many Japanese martial arts refer to rolls and falls or breakfalls as *ukemi,* and indeed a literal translation of ukemi is falls. But certain styles of jujitsu refer to breakfalls as *sutemi*. The distinction is important. Sutemi can mean breakfalls but carries the additional meaning of "to abandon the body or self." Thus the term speaks much more to the flavor of how breakfalls are executed in jujitsu.

This abandoning the body to a fall refers first, and probably most importantly, to a state of mind. When students first learn falling skills, they are taught to do them from crouching or squatting positions. This is the safest way and allows students to gradually build confidence in their ability to do something that is unfamiliar—and that seems to go against common sense. Humans have an almost instinctual wish to avoid the fall or to "right themselves," a need to remain on their feet. Indeed, when unskilled people take a quick accidental fall, they often grab at the ground with their hands and arms, trying to prevent themselves from hitting the ground. More often than not, this results in broken or sprained hands or shoulders. So in jujitsu students initially learn falling skills from close to the ground.

Eventually, though, students get to a point where they can execute aerial breakfalls, or falls that require them to completely leave the ground and flip or twist in the air before coming down. In so doing, they literally "abandon their bodies" from the ground. Or they "abandon" their instinctual drive to remain upright and on their feet. In this sense they "abandon the body" mentally as well as physically. The resultant state of mind becomes critical to their training later on as they learn ever more difficult and sophisticated throwing (*nage*) techniques and counters to nage.

It is also important to distinguish between ukemi and sutemi because at some later point in training, students learn to use sutemi as an actual weapon, and this cannot be accomplished if the student is governed by an instinctual need to remain on the feet or by a fear of falling.

Still another reason for the distinction is that ukemi, as taught in other Japanese martial arts, are often executed without a student's completely leaving the ground. This is not to say that an experienced practitioner of another martial art, say judo, will be less competent at falling. Indeed, an experienced *judoka* (practitioner of judo) can survive any fall as well as can an experienced *jujitsuka* (practitioner of jujitsu). However, jujitsuka are taught that many falls result from fierce combat and that falls may come about as a result of a sudden leaping attack on their legs. They must be able to sustain any impact in such a way as to *seize the combat initiative*. In this way they fall without giving in or giving up. This is why jujitsuka are taught a general falling position that enhances their ability to combat their opponent from the ground.

GROUND-GUARD FIGHTING POSITION

The general ground-guard fighting posture is the falling position for many throws. Note the falling surfaces of the outer calf, thigh, buttock, upper left aspect of the back, and back of the shoulder. Note also the bent legs and position of the hands to cover vital areas. In a left-side fall, the right hand covers the groin and the left hand covers the face. In this position the student can pivot left or right by pushing with the legs, thus continuing to face an opponent who is trying to circle around him or her and making it difficult for the opponent to move forward and attack. This position is easy to assume from any fall that requires a different landing posture. The circumstances of combat will determine if you should maintain this position, once on the ground, or should return to your feet. As a general rule, however, you have more options in combat when you're on your feet.

Ground-guard fighting position

The ground-guard fighting position affords the jujitsuka a sound means for regaining positioning on the feet. To do so, the student sits up in a tight-tuck position, placing the right hand on the knee and the left hand on the ground, close to the left hip. To get up the student then presses down on both hands and swings the left leg up and back, in a pendulum fashion. The buttocks and hips stay low until the rear left foot is firmly planted on the ground. The left foot is perpendicular to the line of the right foot so that when the student stands erect, he or she is in the L-stance.

When pressing down with both hands, it is important to arise vertically, not falling backward into the stance or first planting the rear foot on the ball of the foot. Both of these actions place you off balance and make you vulnerable to any sudden forward rush of the opponent you are facing. The idea here is to have control of your body throughout the actions of getting to your feet. A student

a

b

Standing up from the ground-guard fighting position

under control can propel him- or herself backward from a rushing opponent in the middle of gaining the feet. This is quite different than being off balance, should your opponent decide to rush you.

Finally, note once again the L-stance that is assumed from most kaiten (rolls). This will be covered in the next chapter, but you should understand that although this is a good, sound stance to assume from a fall or roll, it may not be the best exact stance for fighting.

L-stance

THE ART OF FALLING

Mastering the art of falling requires that students learn several basic principles. They must remain relaxed at all times. Impact with the ground requires transferring the momentum of the fall to the ground as fluidly as possible. This is virtually impossible if they remain stiff and rigid. Second, students must learn to exhale upon impact with the ground—or just prior to the impact. If they hold their breath or inhale upon impact, the body stiffens and they experience much more discomfort from the fall. Third, almost all sutemi are accompanied by a firm, yet relaxed, slapping of the ground. The slap robs the fall of some of its momentum but is not intended to stop the fall. In the beginning students are taught a number of drills to reinforce the use of the slap and demonstrate to them that the slap must occur with the proper timing. Otherwise students take up too much of the momentum of the fall with the slapping arm.

a

b

c

Rolling back fall

Students learn that whatever sutemi is to be taken, certain falling surfaces of the body will make contact with the ground: the idea is to distribute the force of the fall evenly across those falling surfaces. In doing so, they come to experience far less discomfort from the fall. At this point, too, they begin to learn and reinforce the idea of body control.

At a more advanced level, jujitsuka must be able to take a breakfall from any sort of attack that takes them off their feet. When students begin to practice nage, they are taught to control the fall of the opponent. But inexperienced students all too often lose control of the opponent, and the person receiving the throw must be able to assume control of the body out of a poorly executed throw. In a typical jujitsu class students are likely to receive in excess of 50 such throws. Just the sheer number of throws can be very wearing, not to mention the fatigue if the throws are poorly executed. So the importance of taking good sutemi becomes critical. Finally, at the more advanced level, the use of the sutemi as a weapon can only be attempted when students can control their bodies while they still are in the air. At the completion of each sutemi, the students immediately correct their body positions to the optimal; then they can assume the ground-guard fighting position.

TECHNIQUE TIPS

1. Stay relaxed.
2. Always exhale when taking a fall.
3. Try to take any fall on as much of the appropriate body surfaces as possible.
4. Tuck your chin as you take falls and look at the ceiling as you land.
5. Keep your mouth closed as you take falls.
6. Watch others taking falls closely; you can learn much from their mistakes or skills.
7. Ask other students what helped them make a breakthrough in falling.
8. Gauge how tensely you hold your abdominal muscles; try to keep them relaxed.
9. Practice rolls and falls as often as possible.
10. Strive to master the spirit of sutemi.

TORI AND UKE

This is a good point at which to introduce some new terminology: *tori* and *uke*. Tori, the defender, executes the technique in response to the attack. Uke, the attacker, is the one on whom the technique is executed. In the case of executing a sequence of multiple techniques, tori and uke may both be attacker and defender. So it might be more accurate to say that tori is the controller at the end of the technique, uke the controlled. Although sutemi are usually practiced individually, they assume the student is in fact uke.

TYPES OF SUTEMI

In most jujitsu styles a student must be able to execute several different types of sutemi because a jujitsuka may be attacked and thrown or knocked down from any direction. We list and describe here the sutemi that students most likely will learn in jujitsu classes.

FALLS

These falls and rolls are usually taught in their most graduated form: that is, the rolls and falls are first taught from squatting or close to the ground—for the students' safety and to allow them to gradually develop confidence in their skills. Eventually they are executed from standing and even from standing and springing positions, thus coming to embody the true nature of sutemi. These more advanced positions more closely approach the ways in which you may be knocked down or thrown in combat.

SIDE FALL

Yoko sutemi, or side fall, begins with the student stepping forward on the right foot. At the same time the right arm cuts sharply to the waist and the left leg lifts sharply upward and to the rear. These motions generate an impulse of momentum to carry the individual through the fall and to a point of commitment to the fall. At this point of commitment, the student learns to tuck the head and shoulders toward the waist and, using the lift from the left leg, spring off the ball of the right foot and flip over a central point—about waist-high—to land on the left side of the body in the ground-guard fighting position. A variation of this fall is the twisting side fall. The fall is executed in the same fashion, but while in the air the jujitsuka twists and lands on the right side of the body (as pictured in photos a-c).

a

b

c

BACK FALL

In *ushiro sutemi*, the back fall, the participant bends the knees slightly, rotates the arms up and backward, and keeps the chest high, upward, and back. The idea is to pivot the body to the rear around a central point, about waist-high. Done correctly, the student lands on the upper back, near the shoulder blades. The landing surface should touch the ground about where the feet were. Care is taken to tuck the chin, to exhale just prior to impact, and to time the slap so as not to catch the full impact through the arms. Visually, the fall should approximate having the legs reaped out (from behind) from under you.

a

b

FRONT FALL

In *mae sutemi*, the front fall, the falling surfaces are the forearms (from the fingertips to the elbows) and the lower, front parts of the thighs (just above the knee joints). The student flexes the knees slightly and springs backward and up, out from underneath the stance. At impact, the arms should be bent at the elbows, vertically aligned in front of the shoulders. The head is turned to either side to avoid hitting the face on the ground. A slight bridge is maintained in the trunk of the body to avoid any impact to the abdomen.

a

b

c

BRIDGE FALL

In *hashi sutemi,* or bridge fall, the falling surfaces are the upper back and the balls of the feet. The student steps forward on the right foot and springs up in the air, flipping over the imaginary central point, much the same as in the side fall. The differences are that both arms make sharp backward, circular movements to generate the impulse to commitment and the student lands neither to the left side nor the right, but on the upper back and the balls of the feet. While in the air the student begins to arch the waist forward, so that at the point of impact the waist and trunk bridge upward. Care is taken to tuck the chin and exhale.

a

b

c

ROLLS

Most schools also include a medley of rolls (*kaiten*) in the curriculum. (These are also included under the general description of sutemi.) Jujitsuka use rolls for several reasons. First, they help close the distance with an opponent. Second, they provide a means of quickly maneuvering to a more defensible location. Third, they provide an unexpected maneuver in the heat of combat that may gain the jujitsuka the tactical advantage. And fourth, they provide the jujitsuka with a means to get over obstacles.

FORWARD ROLL

In *mae kaiten*, the forward roll, the student steps forward onto the right foot, bends both knees, bends forward at the waist, and reaches out and forward with the right arm. The right arm looks as if it is about to circle around an imaginary round object, such as a barrel on its side. This brings the student to a point of commitment, as if the balance is breaking to the front. The head and right shoulder are kept close together, and the entire upper body takes on a rounded appearance. The right arm continues forward and down along the centerline of the body and between the legs. The roll is given momentum with a slight spring from the right foot as it breaks contact with the ground. The body rolls along a vertical centerline beginning from the right forearm to the left, rear hip. During the roll the left leg folds in the same manner as taking a left-side fall, but no slap is given and the momentum is used to carry the student upright to his or her feet. Initially, the student is taught to assume the classic L-stance out of the roll. Eventually, the individual begins to shift from this to a more combative, forward stance.

a

b

c

BACKWARD ROLL

The student begins *ushiro kaiten*, the backward roll, by extending the left arm outward to the side of the body, the palm facing to the rear. At the same time, the right arm crosses the body to go above the left shoulder, the head turns to the left, and the student drops to the left knee. The left knee touches the ground just to the rear of where the left foot was, and the lower left leg folds forward so that the student can sit. As the student sits, she or he quickly lays the upper body back on the ground. The momentum of these actions carries the right leg *over* the left shoulder. Both hands are used to stabilize the body as the right leg reaches out behind the person and the momentum carries him or her to the feet to assume an L-stance. Care should be taken during the roll to bring the right leg over the left shoulder but as close to the midline of the body as possible. This will prevent the student from rolling directly back onto the neck.

a

b

c

SIDE ROLL

In *yoko kaiten*, the side roll, the student crouches low, bends the knees, and tucks the right arm and shoulder across the front of the chest. The motion of the roll is executed perpendicularly to the vertical line of the body. Care is taken to rotate the head, neck, shoulders, and hips at the same time; otherwise the roll will carry the student's body at an odd or uneven angle. The best way to practice this roll is to stand facing a wall. This quickly teaches the individual to roll all parts of the body at the same time.

a

b

c

SPEAR OR DIVING ROLL

In *yari kaiten*, the diving roll, the student takes a running start and launches outward, reaching forward with the arms in the fashion we call "Superman flying." The body is parallel to the ground. The actual rolling is accomplished just as in the forward roll. The difference is that the student is already airborne and has a great deal more momentum.

In first trying this roll, most students add more momentum to the roll than is necessary and begin the tuck-and-roll motion too soon. And these are the keys to this roll. The student must let a good deal of the momentum play itself out *before* beginning the tuck and roll. As the student gains greater experience, she or he can better judge the critical moment to begin the tuck and roll. The student should come out of the roll into the classical L-stance.

Recognize also that the diving roll can be done to cover great distance, to leap high over an obstacle, or for some combination of the two.

a

b

c

Several additional points are important to mention. Although most of the illustrations of the sutemi and kaiten are for the right side only, students should learn and practice them for both sides as appropriate. Practicing the back fall can only be done to the rear, of course, but it can be varied by learning to spring over different obstacles. Many drills and exercises are not shown here, such as doing rolls and falls over people or obstacles.

SELF-DEFENSE TIPS

1. Be aware of the ground surface. Taking a fall on loose bricks may be necessary, but if possible, remain on your feet.
2. Know if you face multiple opponents. Using sutemi as a self-defense strategy or move is usually a mistake when you face more than one opponent.
3. Be aware of your surroundings. Using rolls and falls in self-defense can be enhanced by making use of objects or structures around you.
4. Practice rolls to close both short and long gaps.
5. Practice rolls and falls with an opponent trying to attack you.
6. Practice taking falls, using the momentum to bounce you back to your feet.
7. Know and use the terrain to your advantage. Rolling downhill is much easier, for example, than rolling uphill.

Some rolls and falls can be executed in different sequences to reinforce the idea of transfer of momentum. At some point students practice the rolls and falls without slapping in order to recognize that by relaxing sufficiently, they absorb the shock of falling even without the aid of slapping. At a more advanced stage, students will take falls on a hardwood or concrete surface. This more closely approximates the fall that may be taken in actual combat. The point is that falling and rolling skills continue to be developed as you progress through your training.

This chapter has demonstrated fundamental skills in falling and rolling. In many styles of jujitsu, what you see here may constitute the entire body of sutemi or ukemi. For some styles of jujitsu, these skills are simply what is required to survive throws being practiced in class. For other styles, sutemi is an entire set of skills not just for survival in class but for survival in combat as well. Furthermore, we believe the concept of sutemi to be fundamental—critical to the development of the key building blocks that underlie learning other fighting skills. Remember that through the practice of sutemi you learn how to relax, how to gauge and use momentum, how to breathe properly, how to survive attacks and turn them to your advantage, and how to control yourself. Perhaps most importantly, learning sutemi requires you to face your fears and learn to overcome them.

Sutemi teaches you how to get to the ground and back up from it safely and securely. With the confidence you gain from acquiring these skills, you will be better positioned to practice basic fighting skills on your feet. And that is what awaits you in the next chapter.

CHAPTER

5

STANCES, BLOCKS, STRIKES, AND KICKS

G ood stances ensure that a jujitsuka retains balance and control throughout any combative encounter. Proper blocking allows the jujitsuka to forestall an attack or turn it to advantage. Good striking and kicking allow a jujitsuka to defeat the opponent or create openings to make effective use of other tools that give the advantage in combat, such as throws and groundwork. Although throwing and groundwork are assets, they might also place the jujitsuka in a vulnerable position, however briefly. This is particularly true in the case of multiple opponents. If an opponent can be defeated without giving up the standing position, so much the better. And it is the acquisition of good stance work and striking, kicking, and blocking skills that affords the jujitsuka this opportunity.

STANCES

Good stances allow jujitsuka to retain an upright posture in combat and allow them to move with balance, control, and certainty. Jujitsuka must be able to move in this manner if they hope to take full advantage of their tools and skills. As a general rule, good stances are necessary for jujitsuka to maximize the punishing, damaging, and distracting effects they hope to achieve from striking and kicking. Further, good stance work is absolutely necessary for good blocking, whether to stop, interrupt, or redirect an attack. Finally, sound stances are necessary for the proper execution of throws. Jujitsuka need to move from a balanced position, retain their balance as they move, and continue to be balanced at the conclusion of their movements.

A large number of stances are used in the martial arts. They vary from very low to upright. The legs can be far apart or close together. Weight can be evenly distributed on both legs or heavily placed on either the forward or the rear leg. The martial artist can directly face or turn sideways to an opponent.

All stances have their value according to the style or martial art from which they come and the situation in which they are used. A front-facing stance allows the martial artist to bring all his or her weapons (arms and legs) to bear quickly and to move in several directions for tactical advantage. A sideways stance presents fewer targets to the opponent but limits the variety of attacks and the directions of movement. Low stances also present fewer targets to the opponent and give the martial artist a great deal of power for certain types of strikes, but they reduce the martial artist's ability to move swiftly. The same can be true for stances that favor an uneven distribution of weight. However, there are plenty of exceptions to these observations.

Martial artists who train primarily in fighting from low stances, for instance, may be conditioned to move very swiftly. But there are strengths and limitations to most techniques, and stances are no exception. Well-trained jujitsuka will practice as many stances as possible, though most favor one or two stances as primary tools. Generally speaking, jujitsuka favor upright, front-facing stances because these tend to afford them the most mobility and options, while also allowing them to make the swift, pivoting movements so necessary to executing effective nage.

L- OR T-STANCE

The jujitsuka is in an L- or T-stance. Recall from chapter 4 that this is the stance students first learn to assume out of rolls or getting up from falls. The right leg is forward, the foot pointed toward the opponent. The left leg is to the rear, the foot pointed to the right at a 90-degree angle to the line of the lead foot. The heels of both feet are approximately shoulder-width apart. Rarely is this distance exceeded because it allows for the most even distribution of weight. The knees are slightly bent or flexed and remain directly above the feet. Especially on the lead leg, the foot is turned slightly inward but the knee is turned slightly outward. This position protects the inner edge of the shin bone (the tibia) and presents the outer, more muscular edge to the opponent.

The upper body is turned at the waist to face the opponent. The back is straight, the weight evenly distributed. The right arm is bent at the elbow, pointed at the opponent, wrist straight with the palm up and facing slightly inward. The right elbow is just above waist-level and about four inches away from the torso, with the hand at about midchest level. The left arm is held about two inches from the left side of the torso, with the left forearm parallel to the ground and the left palm facing downward. Both hands are open but relaxed, allowing the fingers to curl slightly. Jujitsuka keep their hands open so they can more easily grab their opponent. The shoulders and upper body remain relaxed and alert. This is a good defensive stance; it allows for effective blocking while not portraying aggressive intent. Jujitsuka are taught to move in this stance in three ways:

1. With short half steps forward and backward.
2. With long steps moving the rear foot to the forward position or the front foot to the rearward position.
3. With half-pivot steps allowing the jujitsuka to face either left or right of the original line of movement.

Gradually these movements become more natural, and students can change direction or distance with ease. Jujitsuka don't like to pick up their feet when moving. They prefer to maintain balance at all times. Sloppy stance work is often characterized by picking up the feet and falling or lurching into the next stance. Since jujitsuka practice foot sweeps, they know that this is the exact moment when one is vulnerable to them. So the moving foot remains in contact with the ground in a sliding motion.

In a variation on the L- or T-stance, the individual faces more forward. The hips and feet face forward. The feet are about shoulder-width apart, from front to back as well as from left to right. Here the left foot is forward, the knees are flexed with the lead foot turned slightly inward, and the lead knee is turned slightly outward. Weight is evenly distributed or slightly heavy on the forward foot. The back is straight. The upper body faces the opponent and is relaxed. The arms are held in front of the body, the elbows bent with the hands about six inches away from the face and at chin-level. In this position the fingers, though allowed to curl more, are not quite in a closed-fist position. The advantage to this variant of stance is its allowing you to face more frontally, which makes it possible to assume the offensive more readily and use your arms and legs more swiftly for striking and kicking.

Variation of the L- or T- stance

TECHNIQUE TIPS

1. Keep the weight properly distributed according to the stance being used.
2. Glide your feet when in motion. Don't pick them up and "clomp" them down.
3. Don't initiate movement by leaning into it.
4. Keep the shoulders over the hips when moving.
5. When shifting your weight, move from the hips.
6. Learn to coordinate your breathing with your movement.
7. Keep the knees slightly bent for better balance and protection.
8. Keep your eyes on your opponent, not on your feet.

FORWARD STANCE

In the forward stance, the right foot is forward, but the body is positioned lower to the ground. Here the distance from the front to the rear foot should be one-and-a-half shoulder widths, though the legs are still just one shoulder-width apart from left to right. Some 60 to 70 percent of the weight is distributed to the front foot. The lead knee and foot are positioned as before, but the rear leg is straighter. Hips face to the front, the back is straight, and the upper body is relaxed. Arms are held the same as in the L- or T-stance. Note that the rear foot is turned as far forward as is possible. In this position the stance is much stronger than if the rear foot was turned outward or to the right. This stance allows for greater power to be applied to strikes and kicks, reduces the mobility slightly, and presents a fairly aggressive posture.

SELF-DEFENSE TIPS

STANCES

1. Choose your stance with care. An L-stance is easily assumed if there is only verbal threat. Use a modified L-stance or forward stance if combat becomes certain.

2. Remember that stances can communicate intent.

3. Remain relaxed but determined.

4. Keep your front facing toward the opponent if possible.

5. Keep your feet on the ground.

BLOCKS, STRIKES, AND KICKS

A wide variety of blocks, kicks, and strikes are found across all styles of jujitsu. Other martial arts such as karate and taekwondo are fundamentally based on striking and kicking, focusing on these aspects in far greater detail. Jujitsuka strive to acquire a broader range of skills and usually don't focus on them to the extent that practitioners of these other styles do; nevertheless these skills are important to jujitsuka as well.

First, assume that an opponent will strike or kick at you in most any combat, whether that person is skilled or not. So you must be able to defend against this type of attack. If your opponent is skilled, this need for defense becomes even more acute. To effectively defend, the jujitsuka must have a thorough understanding of strikes and kicks that comes only from practice of the skills themselves. Further, to practice these skills and counter them each jujitsuka must be able to play the part of uke effectively. That is, the jujitsuka must be a credible attacker in order for the workout partner to learn properly. Secondly, while throws, joint locks, and constriction techniques (which you'll learn about in chapters 7 and 8) are the jujitsuka's "bread and butter," strikes, blocks, and kicks create openings and opportunities that allow the jujitsuka opportunity to use these techniques. And strikes and kicks can be taught with the intent to achieve knockouts (as opposed to gross physical damage) or for the purposes of inducing severe nerve pain. This is in keeping with the jujitsu principle of maximum effect with minimum expenditure of energy.

Blocks can be executed with the intent of stopping an attack with painful suddenness or with the intent of preserving the attacker's momentum. Following the block, the jujitsuka might then turn the attack into an opportunity for a throw and use of constriction technique.

The illustrations here of blocks, strikes, and kicks are only a representative sampling of all such tools that a good jujitsuka would seek to have in his or her arsenal. Further, the situations presented in this chapter are basic ones that need repeated reinforcement and practice, regardless of one's skill level. The given techniques may also be used in different ways depending on the outcome you desire. Remember, flexibility and adaptability are fundamental characteristics of any well-trained jujitsuka.

BLOCKS

A straightforward way to characterize blocks is to call them *hard* or *soft*. Hard blocks generally attempt to stop an attack and or to displace or disrupt the attacker. Hard blocks usually stop or arrest the attacking motion. Soft blocks, on the other hand, generally attempt to redirect the energy of the attack, allowing it to pass by the target. Jujitsuka use this opening for a counterstrike, a throw, or to capture the arm or leg to execute a throw followed by a submission.

TECHNIQUE TIPS

1. When executing solid blocks, put your body into it.
2. When executing passing blocks, be relaxed so that movement comes easily.
3. Blocks create openings—be prepared to take advantage of them.
4. Exhale when executing the block.
5. Let your vision take in the attacker's entire body. Do not look only at the oncoming strike.
6. Observe good principles of movement when executing blocks. Move in a balanced fashion, remaining upright and over your center.

CUTTING BLOCK

In *shuto uke,* or cutting block, the uke throws a roundabout strike with the right hand. Tori executes a cutting block with the left hand. It is called a *cutting block* because of the use of the "knife edge" of the hand. Tori makes contact on the inside of uke's right forearm with the left outside edge of the hand. Tori keeps the arm and body in good, solid vertical alignment and rotates the hand counterclockwise while stepping to the left. This allows tori to bring the entire mass of his or her body into the block, effectively stopping uke's forward momentum. Executed correctly, this block can be very painful to uke's forearm and can break his or her stance. Tori is now inside uke's guard and can counterstrike and execute a throw. Note that tori maintains a good solid stance throughout the execution of the block and keeps the right arm up. From there tori can either block a punch from uke's left hand, deliver a strike to any of several targets, or do both. This would be characterized as a hard block—though it is not as hard as one that makes bone-to-bone contact.

PASSING BLOCK

In *nagashi uke,* the passing block, uke initiates the same attack as in the cutting block. Tori this time folds the left arm at the elbow and covers the left side of the neck and head. Tori steps forward slightly at the same time, which has the effect of protecting the target area and absorbing the power of uke's strike while expending almost no energy. Additionally, tori again moves inside of uke's guard and can deliver a counterstrike as part of the forward movement. The passing aspect of this block results from tori's passing forward into uke's space. Again, tori keeps the right arm up and maintains good balance and posture. This is considered a soft block.

OUTSIDE-ARM BLOCK

In *soto-ude uke,* the outside-arm block, uke delivers a straight strike to tori's face with the closed fist of the right hand. Tori executes a punishing block with the left forearm. The left forearm is brought up to the vertical position and moves across the front of his body, moving from left to right in a tight, powerful movement. At the same time that tori's arm moves from left to right, the forearm rotates clockwise and the left hand is held in a closed fist. This powerful block contacts the outside of uke's right forearm, moving it off the line of attack, and leaves tori in a strong position to execute techniques against the right corner or dead angle of uke's body. This maneuver has the additional advantage of displacing uke and making it harder for uke to strike at tori with the left hand. This is considered a hard block.

PASSING OR PARRYING BLOCK

In this version of *nagashi uke,* the passing or parrying block, uke initiates the same attack. Tori blocks by catching uke's strike with his or her open left hand and simply redirecting it. Here timing is important. Tori's left hand actually moves along the line of uke's strike, intercepting the strike before it reaches the target. Tori's hand doesn't clutch or grab uke's arm but simply moves (or deflects) it, with gentle pressure, off its original line. At the same time, tori moves slightly to the left while turning his or her body slightly to the right. Properly executed, the momentum of uke's punch is preserved—and finding no target, it is likely to break uke's balance forward. This leaves tori again outside uke's guard, on the right corner or dead angle of uke's body. However, tori's advantage is far greater, and uke is left open to far more attacks and counterstrikes. If uke is not well trained in striking, he or she is likely to be so far off balance that tori will have little or no difficulty throwing uke to the ground. It takes a great deal of practice to master the proper timing and movement that is required for this type of soft or passing block (also called a parry).

DOWNWARD BLOCK

In *gedan uke,* or downward block, uke attacks with a right leg, frontally snap-kicking to tori's groin. Leaving the left foot in place, tori drops the right leg back and assumes a low, forward stance. As the kick begins, tori crosses the forearms, fists clenched, palms facing rearward. As the right leg drops back, tori rotates the forearms so the palms are facing toward the floor. This is done with a powerful, forward thrust of the arms. The thrust of the arms must be timed to coincide with the drop of the body into the forward stance.

By dropping into the forward stance, tori moves the groin and abdomen out of the range of the kick. By rotating and thrusting the crossed forearms forward, tori adds a great deal of power to this block, but this action must be done with the drop of the body in order to add the downward movement of the body mass to the block. Using only the arms usually reduces the effectiveness of the block. Executed correctly, however, tori stops uke's snap kick and is in the position to grab uke's leg and throw him or her off balance. However, tori must move quickly before uke has a chance to withdraw the kick and attack again. This is a hard block.

DOWNWARD-PASSING BLOCK

This next block is called *gedan-nagashi uke,* or downward-passing block. Uke again attacks with a right, front snap kick to the groin. Tori steps off the line of the attack to the left and forward, turning slightly to the right and facing toward uke. At the same time tori's left arm, the palm facing uke's right leg, moves in a downward arc across the front of his or her own body. Executed correctly, tori redirects uke's kick and removes the target from the line of attack. Tori is now on the outside right corner of uke's body and in a good position to attack. If the timing is good on the passing block (parry), tori can catch uke's right leg in the crook of the right arm

SELF-DEFENSE TIPS

BLOCKS

1. Once you have executed a block, keep moving to seize the initiative.
2. Be aware that multiple strikes may come at you, so multiple blocks may be necessary.
3. If you are hit or the block was not completely successful, you must continue to gain the initiative.
4. A block alone will not defeat your opponent. Strike and attack as soon afterward as you can.
5. Do not let your attention be captured by the attack.

and easily throw uke. This is a soft block, and it requires good timing.

Remember that there are many types of blocks and attacks. How well a jujitsuka responds to an attack will depend on the type of attack, skill of the attacker, and the situation. More importantly, the jujitsuka's response will depend upon how much he or she has practiced the various blocks.

STRIKES

As with stances, a wide variety of strikes have been developed across different styles and martial arts. Nearly every surface of the hand can accomplish a strike of some sort, and many other variations of striking are done with the elbows and knees. In most martial arts, striking with the hand is accomplished with a closed fist that is rotated horizontally so the palm side is down and the back of the hand is parallel to the floor.

The primary striking surface spans the two large knuckles of the index and middle finger. Care is taken to keep the arm straight, elbow down, and wrist straight. The strike usually starts within the width of the body and angles inward toward the opponent's centerline. A good, solid stance is necessary to give this strike power. A variation on this is to strike with the

a

b

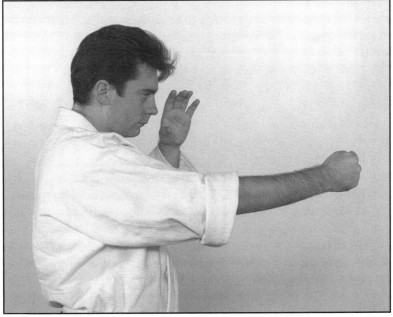

Striking with the fist in the *(a)* horizontal and *(b)* vertical position

fist in the vertical position, observing good stance and body alignment.

A well-trained jujitsuka learns and practices as many striking methods as possible. The more tools you have, the greater your options for response. Traditionally, strikes in jujitsu are called *atemi*. Atemi embody a variety of strikes designed to cause crippling pain or unconsciousness by hitting a specific target area with the surface of your hand, elbow, or knee. The descriptions we give here are not all-inclusive; there is a lot more to atemi than you'll read about here.

The difference between atemi and other striking can best be shown by example. If a jujitsuka *strikes* the opponent in the ribs with the widely used closed-fist strike, he or she may hope to break the ribs, knock the breath from the opponent's body, possibly knock the opponent from his or her stance, and cause a great deal of pain. Using atemi, however, the jujitsuka would attempt with a single bent knuckle to hit a spot in the ribs about the diameter of a quarter. The jujitsuka would be aiming for a specific nerve that, when struck, would cause the opponent's chest muscles to spasm, rendering the opponent unable to breathe. If the jujitsuka did nothing else, there is a fair chance that the opponent would quickly collapse and fall unconscious. The advantage to atemi is that it is subtle, requires little power, and can be delivered in the midst of another movement. The disadvantages, on the other hand, are that it requires very good timing, precise target placement, years of practice, and a sound understanding of anatomy and physiology. Even so, some techniques of atemi are not quite so specialized.

PALM-HEEL STRIKES

Tori strikes uke with an open-handed, heel of the palm strike to uke's chin. This sort of striking favors an open-handed fighting stance, such as the L-stance commonly used by jujitsuka. As tori blocks uke's right hand with the left arm, tori steps into uke's center on the right foot. At the same time tori drives the right palm up along uke's centerline, to catch uke's chin with the heel of the right palm. Done correctly, this strike is very hard to detect in time and will result in a knockout.

The same situation occurs again, but tori now drives a right palm heel strike directly from his or her waist to uke's nose on an upward angle. This is a stunning blow and usually fills uke's eyes with tears, causing temporary blindness.

Tori blocks uke's right-hand roundabout strike with a left cutting block. Immediately after executing the block, tori turns slightly to the left and slaps the left side of uke's jawbone with an open right palm. Tori makes contact with the left edge of uke's jaw in a downward motion. This strike is easily executed after the block, gaining its power from the downward turning motion of tori's body. The palm and hand are relaxed.

a

b

c
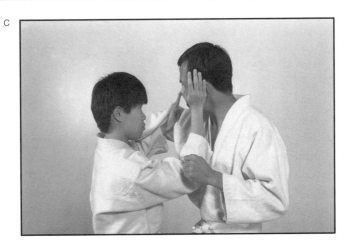

ELBOW STRIKE

Jujitsuka strongly favor elbow and knee strikes because they must be executed close into the opponent's body, which is where jujitsuka feel most comfortable. After striking uke's chin with the heel of the palm, tori bends his or her elbow and, in a continuation of the upward motion, again strikes uke's chin or throat with the tip of the elbow.

KNEE STRIKE

Uke is holding tori in a frontal bear hug, arms pinned to the side. Instead of trying to break the grip, tori pulls uke closer and drives the upper side of the right knee into uke's groin. Depending on the situation, tori may repeat this motion several times. Note that all of tori's weight is shifted to the left leg while striking. To keep good balance, tori keeps a straight back and the left knee bent. In this case, the striking surface is the lower thigh, just above the knee.

TECHNIQUE TIPS

1. Exhale when executing the strike.
2. Stay relaxed. Tense only at the point of impact.
3. Observe good movement principles when striking.
4. Coordinate movements to bring the entire body into the strike.
5. Be sure to strike with only the intended body surface.
6. Focus on the intended target area.
7. Do not overextend the strike.

KICKS

Well-trained jujitsuka attempt to train in as many kicking techniques as possible. As a general rule, however, jujitsuka don't like to find themselves standing on one leg for very long. Neither do they like to do anything that might compromise balance (unless it is in the act of a powerful throwing motion). Consequently, jujitsu kicks are usually low, almost never above the waist. Targets are usually the feet, knees, and groin.

FRONT SNAP KICK

Tori executes a left, front snap kick to uke's right knee. The kick is executed by tori picking the left knee up to just below waist level. In a very rapid motion tori extends the left lower leg forward, extending the foot straight while curling the toes backward. The striking surface is the ball of the foot, which makes contact at uke's knee joint. The lower leg is then retracted almost more rapidly than it was extended—this is what gives this kick its snapping appearance.

Tori *never fully extends* the kicking leg to avoid damaging knee ligaments. This overextension is a common mistake with beginners. Note, too, that tori bends the right knee and keeps the back straight to maintain balance. Throughout the kick, tori's arms are also kept up in a proper guard position to help maintain balance. Do not thrust the arms forward.

TECHNIQUE TIPS

1. Exhale when executing the kick.

2. Do not overextend the kick.

3. When posting your weight on one leg, keep that knee bent to maintain balance.

4. Kick with the intended body surface only.

5. Focus on kicking the intended target.

6. Don't lean away from the kick; coordinate your entire body into the kick.

STOMP

Tori is again being held in a frontal bear hug by uke. This time tori raises the right knee slightly and, in a powerful downward motion, drives the heel of the right foot onto the top of uke's left foot. While this kick is more properly called a *stomp*, in most jujitsu styles it is still considered a kick. Executed correctly, this stomping kick will likely break the fragile bones in uke's left foot. Tori may quickly remove the foot and withdraw or may leave the foot in place and execute a throw.

Example of the stomp.

SELF-DEFENSE TIPS

STRIKES AND KICKS

1. Be prepared to deliver more than one strike or kick.

2. In combat, strikes and kicks are often only partially successful. Move to the next strike—don't stop.

3. Use strikes and kicks to create openings for throws or finishing techniques.

4. Be aware of the changing situation and deliver the strike or kick that is appropriate for the situation.

5. Strikes and kicks can be delivered simultaneously with blocks.

6. Remain calm when striking and kicking; trying too hard can make you tense.

7. Maintain good posture when striking and kicking. Don't lose balance or overcommit.

It is worth repeating as a final word about strikes, kicks, blocks, and stances that jujitsuka train in all the styles and techniques they can. Situations often dictate how and what to use. Close-in combat favors certain techniques over others, but so does the size and nature of the jujitsuka's body. After a great deal of training, an individual will find the most appropriate techniques. Remember that if a given instructor or style favors certain techniques only, that doesn't necessarily render them invalid. Experienced instructors will have good reasons for teaching the techniques they do. Jujitsuka tend to favor lower kicks, open-handed and atemi type striking, softer blocks or parries, and upright, mobile stances.

CHAPTER

ESCAPES AND COUNTERS

The techniques students first use to practice the principle of leverage in jujitsu are known as *yawara*. The principle of leverage is extremely important to the proper execution of jujitsu, and its use can be found throughout the entire body of jujitsu techniques. Leverage is what allows a smaller or weaker individual to overcome or at least counter a larger or stronger opponent. It is first learned by practicing escapes from and counters to simple grabs.

Not all styles of jujitsu call these techniques yawara. Some simply refer to them as escapes or counters. Some styles don't single out these techniques at all but simply include them as part of a sequence of several techniques. Nonetheless, experienced sensei will utilize these techniques to illustrate the importance of leverage.

When one person grabs another, the natural response is to pull away. This instinctive attempt to escape may be successful if the person grabbed is larger or stronger. But what happens if the person is smaller or weaker? Pulling away through using sheer strength is less likely to succeed. If strength is used, the attacker is less likely to be discouraged from grabbing the person again. But by the use of leverage a victim is able to escape in a nearly effortless manner, which is likely to confound if not discourage the attacker. The victim can also use leverage to defeat the grab and counter it with a technique or series of techniques that will put the attacker at a disadvantage.

In the techniques we illustrate in this chapter, tori and uke stand facing each other. Usually, uke initiates the attack by grabbing tori. In some techniques, tori simply does a yawara technique to uke. Techniques practiced in this fashion, however, allow students to learn the mechanics of the technique without the distraction of being attacked in a more realistic way.

As learners become more familiar and capable of executing the technique, the context is broadened to allow other movements, such as striking, kicking, tackling, and so on. In other words, students progress to more and more realistic situations. Some sensei, to the contrary, prefer to teach a given technique in a realistic situation from the beginning. There are pros and cons to each way of introducing students to a particular technique. Ultimately, good sensei will get students to the necessary level of proficiency no matter their means of introduction.

Understand, too, that the techniques shown here are by no means the only ways to defeat a given grab or attack. Usually students learn one way initially, but eventually learn dozens of variations. By combining these variations with striking, kicking, and assorted other responses, a well-trained jujitsuka can effectively deal with most attackers.

This is, indeed, one of the jujitsuka's greatest strengths. When attacked, jujitsuka can respond with a multitude of techniques—embodying the *ju* in jujitsu, that is, the flexibility. If a response isn't working, jujitsuka don't try to force it; they simply move on to a different technique. It is said, "Push when pulled and pull when pushed." Don't oppose strength with strength. This principle resurfaces over and over again.

SELF-DEFENSE TIPS

Escapes and Counters

1. When attempting an escape or counter, maintain good posture, remain relaxed, and keep your head up.

2. Maintain good awareness; don't look at the technique—*feel* it.

3. If it fails to work, don't stop but instead move on to another technique.

4. If your intent is to escape, do so. Step back and gain a defensive posture—or leave the area entirely.

5. If you counter, decide quickly what you intend to do. Either further subdue or incapacitate your opponent. Don't just stand there and hold "a tiger by the tail."

6. Be aware of the possibility that there are multiple opponents. Either quickly incapacitate your initial opponent or shove one opponent at the next to create a diversion so you can leave the area.

7. Remember that most techniques can be countered—and knowledgeable opponents also know this.

8. Remember that though the pain resulting from well-executed yawara may subdue the opponent, in some cases it will cause further rage. Be prepared for this.

9. Pain is not experienced the same way when the opponent is drugged, drunk, or stimulated by adrenaline.

SINGLE-HAND ESCAPE

In *katate hazushi* uke grabs tori in a mirror-image grip, just above the wrist. Mirror image means the right on left or the left on right—as opposed to a cross grip, where the right is on right or the left is on left. Tori rotates the left palm downward, parallel to the floor. Then tori steps in slightly on the left foot and collapses the left elbow forward, as if to touch uke's elbow. Next tori pivots partially to the right, removing the wrist from uke's grip. By rotating the palm downward, uke's hand is positioned so that when the elbow collapses forward, tori's forearm acts as a lever against the weakest part of uke's grip. Thus the escape requires little effort at all. The movement gives the leverage additional power and places tori offline and facing uke's dead angle. Throughout, tori keeps the other hand up in the guard position, centering the eyes on uke's upper chest. In the photo, the right hand remains down so the technique is more clearly illustrated.

a

b

SINGLE-HAND ESCAPE AND COUNTER

In *tekubi tori,* uke again grabs tori in a mirror-image grip. Tori steps offline to the left again, but this time rotates the left hand palm up. With the right hand, tori reaches under uke's right hand and grabs around the base of the thumb. Tori then rotates the left hand palm down and grabs the outside edge of uke's hand. While holding this grip, tori steps and turns farther to the left and rotates uke's hand counterclockwise. The painful pressure this brings to uke's hand and wrist forces uke to fall to the ground. Thus, tori not only defeats uke's grab, but, using the principle of leverage, counters the grab and throws uke to the ground. Throughout, tori maintains good balance and power and remains in a position to release uke or follow with a kick, a submission technique, or both.

a

b

These escape and counter techniques illustrate the manner in which jujitsuka are often taught yawara. First they learn to escape the grab; then they learn to escape by countering the grab and assuming control. As jujitsuka progress, they learn appropriate submission techniques. Thus jujitsuka learn, incrementally, how to connect techniques together in flowing maneuvers. But the fundamental lesson of yawara is learning to make use of the principle of leverage. Another way to state this is that by learning to apply leverage to the joints of the extremities (arms and legs), jujitsuka find they are able to control uke's body and assume control of the situation.

FINGERHOLD ESCAPE

In the fingerhold escape *(yubi tori hazushi),* uke grabs the four fingers of tori's right hand with the left. To escape, tori steps back on the right foot and draws the right hand to the right hip. This draws uke's hand away from the body, thus giving tori greater leverage and uke less. Tori raises the right hand to shoulder height and steps back on the left foot, relaxes the grabbed fingers, and thrusts the heel of the right palm forward. This should effect tori's escape, who can then step back to once more resume a defensive posture. The technique illustrates how leverage is greater when you get closer to the body. Uke's leverage decreases as the hand is drawn away from his or her body. Consider this as a refinement of the leverage principle, one that is important to understand.

a

b

FOUR-FINGERS TECHNIQUE

This four-fingered technique *(moro yubi tori)* illustrates what uke would hope to accomplish with the previous technique we described. Tori now *initiates* the action by grabbing the fingers of uke's right hand with the left. Tori pushes uke's hand downward while bending uke's fingers upward. This locks the finger joints on uke's hand, as well as stretching and tightening the attached tendons. Tori pivots clockwise 90 degrees and, at the same time, turns uke's hand clockwise. Grasping the back of uke's right elbow with the right hand, tori steps up next to uke, so they are facing the same direction. Tori then lifts uke's fingers directly upward, while keeping uke's elbow locked. This is an extremely painful hold, and to complete it tori turns to the left, making uke try to keep up with the movement (this is sometimes called a "come along"). Again, the use of leverage when applied to the joints of the extremities can cause great pain, break the opponent's balance, and give the jujitsuka control of the situation. Tori has a variety of other effective and safe ways to release or further control uke.

a

b

c

TECHNIQUE TIPS

1. Escapes and counters are executed with good leverage, not pushing or pulling.

2. The entire body is brought into motion to attain leverage, not only the extremities.

3. Exhale when executing the escape or counter.

4. Observe good body posture as you execute the technique.

5. If a technique doesn't work, be prepared to move into another one.

6. Keep your free hand or arm up to block.

7. Find the weakest part of the grab and attack it.

8. Move to reduce exposure to strikes and kicks.

9. Move from the hips.

10. Use an open gaze, focusing on no particular body part, to see your entire opponent.

At this stage of study jujitsuka begin to understand the mechanics of human anatomy. For example, by bending finger joints in the direction opposite their natural bend all joints between the fingers will lock, tendons will tighten, nerves will be pressured, and the resulting pain and leverage will cause the opponent to move the way you wish. Understanding human anatomy gives the jujitsuka a huge advantage. So the wisest sensei will begin to instruct their students early on about human anatomy and physiology, and they themselves should have commanding knowledge of these subjects.

Yawara teaches jujitsuka that leverage can be used to escape or control the opponent. Jujitsuka come to understand how basic structural human anatomy makes this leverage so powerful. If jujitsuka use this awareness to further their knowledge of human structural anatomy, they can more quickly grasp how learning to use leverage makes throwing possible—and they gain a distinct advantage over their opponents. In throwing, the entire body is used to gain leverage, a phenomenon we look at in the next chapter.

CHAPTER

THROWS

Nage is the heart and soul of jujitsu. Nage is, literally, throwing technique. The premise of nage is that as hard as you can hit a person, it's likely you can cause far more hurt by throwing the person to the ground. While the total scope of jujitsu extends far beyond how much you can hurt a person, it is and was about the need to survive in combat. Throwing provides jujitsuka with an enormously powerful weapon to ensure survival in combat. Not only does throwing cause an opponent greater damage, but it can put the opponent at a far greater disadvantage strategically.

For the most part, throws are executed from close proximity to the opponent's body. Throws that meet this criteria are generally known as *tai waza*, or body techniques. Remembering the previous chapter on yawara, it is not hard to imagine how locking a wrist joint, for instance, can allow the jujitsuka to complete a throw. This sort of throwing makes use of all the principles of both yawara and nage, but fundamentally nage is learning to use one's entire body to lever the opponent's entire body to the ground. As such, nage is usually executed from close in to the opponent.

In judo, various throws are often categorized according to what part of the body is used to execute the throw. For instance, *tai waza* is using the entire body to perform the throw, and *ashi waza* is using the feet to effect reaps or sweeps. *Reaping throws* get their name because the action is similar to that of a sickle that a farmer might use to harvest grain by hand. The motion follows a curved path, as does the blade of a sickle, and moves are executed with sharp and powerful movements of the legs. *Sweeping throws* are also executed with the legs, but there the motion is more like that of the sweeping motion of a broom. Various styles of jujitsu use this same system of categorization. Others simply refer to throws according to which body part the leverage is applied.

KATA

Nage might also be considered the heart and soul of judo, which, you may recall from the history chapter, was derived from the older forms of jujitsu. In both judo and jujitsu, nage is usually first practiced as *kata*. Kata begins with two practitioners facing each other, standing still and gripping each other's *gi*, or jacket. Motion is generated by tori moving some portion of uke's body in a prescribed sequence. This serves to break uke's balance, and it positions tori to leverage uke's body to the ground. The breaking of uke's balance is called *kuzushi*. Once kuzushi has been achieved, tori has the advantage of leverage and, with minimal effort, should be able to put uke on the ground. This leverage is what allows a 95-pound man or woman to throw a 250-pound individual. This kata form of practice is constant throughout one's study of jujitsu, and it allows jujitsuka to understand and incorporate the mechanics of each throw.

Eventually, each throw is practiced from movement. Movement allows a student to concentrate on blending his or her throwing movements with the movement of uke's body to create leverage. The emphasis here is not on creating kuzushi from stillness, but on attaining kuzushi by blending your own movement with your opponent's. Timing thus becomes a key factor.

Look at it this way: in any throwing movement there is a sweet spot where tori can leverage uke to the ground to the greatest effect and using the least effort. Observing this movement, one can see that timing is of utmost importance in throwing.

FREE PLAY

Timing becomes even more critical in *randori*. Randori, a term coined in judo, may be referred to as *free play*. That is, movement is no longer kata-like in nature, but results from two jujitsuka trying to throw each other in a competitive free play. In randori the students are learning to apply nage in a rapidly changing scenario, one closer to realistic combat situations.

Remember as you practice nage in randori, timing becomes critical because opportunities appear and disappear so rapidly. As jujitsuka progress through training, other techniques such as striking, kicking, joint locking, and ground fighting (see chapter 8) are incorporated to even more closely simulate combat. However, randori and the static kata practice of nage never leave the jujitsuka's training regimen. Constant practice of nage allows jujitsuka to develop and hone their sense of the body and timing so that it becomes second nature, almost a subconscious phenomenon, to apply nage and sense the openings for it.

One need only be uke for a master to experience the almost magical way in which such an expert can effortlessly throw an opponent, regardless of what the individual does. But never forget that this does not come from 10 easy lessons—rather it results from many, many years of serious practice.

Remember, too, that not all styles of jujitsu teach nage in this fashion. Many simply incorporate nage as one of several actions in a sequence. By practicing a sequence over and over again, in response to several different attacks, the jujitsuka begins to apply the sequence to almost any scenario. This can be a highly effective method of training, particularly when the object is to prepare a student for situations requiring self-defense. But the greatest masters of nage get there by the regular kata practice of nage— in addition to sequential strings of techniques and self-defense applications.

OFF-BALANCING YOUR OPPONENT

We must add another observation: remember that kuzushi is the breaking of the opponent's balance. Once the balance is broken, a

SELF-DEFENSE TIPS

1. If a throw doesn't work, don't force it. Move to another throw.

2. Maintain good balance as you execute a throw. Throwing yourself to ground unexpectedly may cause you to lose whatever advantage that nage gives you.

3. Be prepared, however, to follow through with submission techniques or finishing strikes.

4. If multiple opponents are present, then finish with striking, to allow you to stay on your feet.

jujitsuka can usually throw the opponent with ease. Jujitsu master Henry Okazaki once said, "To move a boat on land requires the strength of ten men, but if the boat is in the water, one man can move it with ease." Kuzushi is like putting the boat in the water.

Kuzushi can be achieved in a number of ways. From a resting position, one achieves it by either pulling or pushing in any number of directions. Applying pain either through striking, kicking, or nerve pressure holds can cause uke to move, and the movement itself creates the kuzushi. If nage is practiced from movement, it is a matter of pushing or pulling as well—but this is done to redirect or accelerate the momentum already there from the movement.

As before, striking, kicking, or nerve pressure holds applied at the proper point and time will again create kuzushi. In sum, nage is the act of throwing one's opponent. This results from the proper application of leverage, either with the entire body or with some part of the body applied to the opponent. To make nage effective one must achieve kuzushi, or unbalancing of the opponent. Kuzushi has to occur at the proper moment, and thus timing becomes critical, whether nage is practiced from movement or rest.

TECHNIQUE TIPS

1. Good nage begins with good kuzushi.
2. Learn to move from your hips.
3. Maintain good posture when executing a throw.
4. Identify and employ the correct leverage when executing a throw.
5. Exhale as you execute the throw.
6. After the throw, return to a sound body position or execute a submission technique.
7. Once you learn the components of a throw, practice them to achieve continuous flow.
8. Practice nage from kata, movement, and self-defense applications.

SHOULDER-LEVERING TECHNIQUE

The shoulder-levering technique is also called *seoi nage*. Tori and uke stand facing each other in the standard beginning position, gripping each other's gi (or jacket), also in the standard fashion. Tori begins by first pulling uke's right arm forward and upward to achieve kuzushi. At the same time tori steps forward on the right foot and pivots counterclockwise while keeping the pull constant on uke's arm. As tori steps forward, the knees bend and the right shoulder fits into uke's right armpit while the right hand grasps uke's gi at the shoulder. At this point tori is facing the same direction as uke. Uke is pulled forward against uke's back, the right arm over tori's shoulder and held firmly to tori's back. Uke is now off balance.

Tori finishes the throw by bending sharply at the waist and levering uke over the back to the ground. Tori does not let go of uke's arm, even though the throw is completed, but regains a strong upright posture and then decides whether to follow with a submission technique or simply let go and move back into a defensive posture. In a real combat situation tori may execute the throw and let go of uke. If uke doesn't know how to fall properly, this will likely result in serious injury. But in practices tori retains the grip on uke's sleeve to ensure a proper fall—and in case a following technique is to be applied. This throw is a standard shoulder-levering technique. Realize that there are many ways to throw seoi nage; this is but one of them.

In jujitsu we have a saying "What you see is what you get." This means that to perform any good nage, all the principles we have outlined must be observed. In some jujitsu schools it has been observed that uke jumps into the throw for tori. This is not true or good nage. Tori learns nothing about the principles of good nage if uke leaps into the throw. So beware of jujitsu schools that practice this way. Seek out schools and sensei that require you to learn good nage through the principles we have outlined. It may take longer for a student to learn this way, but the object should be to learn well, not quickly.

a

b

c

HIP-LEVERING THROW

In the hip-levering throw, or *ogoshi*, tori and uke stand facing each other with a standard gi hold. Tori begins the throw by stepping in on his or her right foot, dropping the right arm around and behind uke's back, and pulling uke's right arm up and forward to achieve kuzushi. This loads most of uke's weight onto the right foot. Tori pivots counterclockwise until facing the same direction as uke, but as tori executes this pivot, the knees are bent so that tori's pelvis is lower than uke's. Tori extends the right hip slightly beyond uke's right hip. While continuing to draw uke's right arm forward, tori loads uke onto the right hip, straightens both legs, and bends forward at the waist. This levers uke over tori and to the ground. As before, tori keeps control of uke's arm and stands upright into a stable stance. This is a hip-levering throw, and it works because tori's center (gravity) gets below uke's center and gives tori the leverage to throw uke to the ground. As before, there are several ways to throw ogoshi. This is but one of them.

a

b

c

LEG-REAPING THROW

In the leg-reaping throw, or *osoto gari*, tori and uke face each other with standard grips on the gi. Tori steps forward on the left foot, even with and just to the left of uke's right foot. At the same time, tori leads uke to the right with the right and left hands, so that uke's weight rests mostly on the right foot, thus achieving kuzushi. Note that when tori steps to the left, tori's left knee also bends slightly to give the stance greater stability. Tori then brings the right leg forward and past uke's right leg and, keeping the right leg straight, swings it up and past uke.

Next tori brings the straightened right leg backward, in a forceful reaping motion. When the right calf makes contact with uke's right calf, tori bends forward at the waist and throws uke backward to the ground. If tori bends at the waist before calf meets calf, the throw is unlikely to succeed. This is a leg-reaping throw. Again, there are several variations of osoto gari.

a

b

c

d

We have described three examples of nage found in most styles of jujitsu. There are many more nage to be learned, and each separate nage has several variations. Remember that nage is about using all or most of the body to acquire leverage over one's opponent. Nage works because of this leverage principle and by acquiring a good sense of timing as to when to apply leverage and kuzushi. Ultimately, nage should be practiced from standing kata, moving kata, randori, and positions of self-defense in order for the jujitsuka to attain a high degree of proficiency.

Well-executed nage can finish the opponent, especially if uke doesn't know how to fall properly. But jujitsuka don't rely on this happening; rather they have a full body of submission or ground-fighting techniques to apply when the opponent hits the ground. These techniques will be the subject of the next chapter.

CHAPTER

8

GROUND FIGHTING

It has been said that 90 percent of all fights end up on the ground. *Shime* are the techniques of jujitsu designed for ground fighting and submission. Many of the shime techniques resemble moves found in the various styles of competitive wrestling. But whereas the moves in competitive wrestling were designed to constrict an opponent to achieve a pin, *shime waza* (shime techniques) originally developed to disable the opponent by causing serious bodily harm. These techniques usually attacked a body joint, cut off air or blood flow, or achieved disabling nerve damage. Jujitsu developed in an era when combat was most often a matter of life or death. It is likely that the emphasis was on utterly defeating the opponent, more than simply getting the opponent to submit. Even so, submission might be the goal if one wanted to capture an opponent or render the opponent immobile.

Some current jujitsu styles today don't distinguish whether a technique is used to disable or defeat. But the more complete styles have layers of understanding about technique, teaching shime first as a way to get the opponent to give up and later as a means to cripple the person. Shime, therefore, is often an area where jujitsuka first begin to consider how seriously to harm an opponent. Defeating an obnoxious drunk in a bar doesn't merit a crippling response, but defending against a knife-wielding attacker bent on killing you might indeed justify it.

In any case, shime waza are first practiced as submission arts in the dojo. As the jujitsuka becomes more skilled, improved technique will allow achieving what is intended without seriously harming the workout partner. Here, the concept of control enters into training. Control can refer to the controlling of your opponent, but equally or even more importantly to controlling yourself. These techniques can cause serious, though unintended, harm. Jujitsuka must strive to control not only their strength but also their emotions.

RESUSCITATION ARTS

In shime, jujitsuka begin to broaden their understanding of human anatomy. Since the shime arts are usually designed to attack specific joints, nerves, and blood or air pathways, a knowledge of human anatomy allows students to apply techniques more effectively. For example, by knowing exactly where the carotid artery is most vulnerable to constriction, jujitsuka can vastly increase the effectiveness of a blood choke as an incapacitating technique. In the most complete jujitsu systems, shime usually is where the jujitsuka is also first taught *kappo* or *katsu* (resuscitation arts).

If two jujitsuka are practicing choking techniques and one of them actually is rendered unconscious, katsu can be applied swiftly to assure revival. Knowing human anatomy and physiology greatly enhance this capability. Resuscitation is usually the responsibility of the sensei, but if two jujitsuka are practicing on their own, they should learn a method of resuscitation. So training in shime represents not only a new level of achievement and understanding for the jujitsuka but also a new level of responsibility.

Many contemporary systems of jujitsu don't have a knowledge of kappo or katsu. In traditional systems, this was closely guarded information and was passed on to only the most trusted of students. Therefore, more modern eclectic systems usually lack these arts. In today's "I will sue you" environment, it is usually wise to summon appropriate medical authorities to deal with injury. But such medical aid was not available in Japan's feudal era. Thus martial systems developed and closely guarded their body of healing arts. So jujitsu systems that possess these arts are most likely derived from traditional, classical systems.

In practicing shime, the jujitsuka must be alert to the signals of the workout partner. Techniques that bend or stretch joints, render a partner unconscious, or cause severe nerve pain can quickly become serious injuries. Jujitsuka signal each other by tapping each other or the floor twice. This is a universal signal that the technique has been successful and need go no further. When the technique renders the jujitsuka unable to signal, they say "*matte*," which means *wait* but most often effectively sends the signal to stop.

CATEGORIES OF SHIME

Judo actually refers to shime *waza* as *gatame waza*, which means hold-down or grappling techniques. These are then broken down into *shime waza* (choking techniques), *osaekomi waza* (pinning techniques), and *kansetsu waza* (joint-locking techniques). Although this categorization may or may not be present in jujitsu systems, it is useful for recognizing the actions that the various techniques are designed for. Some techniques actually accomplish more than one action. The techniques that follow will illustrate this.

In *kata* practice, shime are usually applied after a throw. Jujitsuka will retain a hold on their partners so that following shime can more easily be achieved. But realize that shime may be applied to an opponent no matter how he or she gets to the ground. This is especially true in self-defense situations. As jujitsuka become more proficient in shime waza, they begin to apply them from all sorts of takedowns, as well as to nage.

CROSS-BODY HOLD

In *juji gatame*—cross-body hold—tori has thrown uke to the ground, retaining a hold of uke's right sleeve with the left hand. Almost at the exact moment that uke hits the ground on the back, tori steps over uke's arm with the left leg and drops to both knees, trapping uke's left arm between the legs. Tori squeezes uke's left arm between the legs to retain control and lets go with the left hand. Tori lies across uke's chest, perpendicular to the length of uke's body, pinning uke's back to the floor, and grabs uke's left wrist with the right hand. Tori stretches out to full length and straightens and pins uke's arm to the floor, palm facing up. At the same time tori's left arm crosses under uke's left elbow in a figure-4 configuration. This allows tori to apply a painful arm bar against uke's left arm, while pinning uke to the ground. At this point, tori can apply this hold as a painful submission technique or choose to break or dislocate uke's elbow. To release, tori comes to both knees, while retaining control of both of uke's arms and executes a forward roll across uke's body, coming to the feet, turning to face uke, and assuming a good defensive stance.

a

b

c

d

e

TECHNIQUE TIPS

1. Shime arts require a sound understanding of human anatomy.
2. Learn shime arts by themselves; then practice them from nage or as self-defense.
3. Precision can be very important in shime; learn the fine points thoroughly!
4. When practicing ground arts, remember to keep your body low to the ground.
5. Ground fighting can be very exhausting, so learn to conserve energy.
6. Don't try to outmuscle your opponent; instead cultivate good technique.
7. Practice moving from one ground art to another to develop flow.
8. Employ your whole body in executing shime arts.
9. Practice ground fighting regularly.

REVERSE-CROSS CONSTRICTION

The following technique is called *gyaku juji shime,* or reverse-cross constriction. Tori has thrown uke to the ground so that the opponent is laying flat on the back. Tori retains hold of uke's right arm with the left hand. As soon as uke hits the ground, tori steps over uke's body with the right leg, drops to both knees, and straddles uke's hips. At the same time tori reaches high on uke's right lapel with the right hand, palm facing down and thumb underneath, firmly grasping the lapel. Tori then reaches for uke's left lapel, left arm over right, and attains a similar grip. Tori hunches down, head close to uke's head, and in a scissors motion pushes both elbows outward and down to choke uke's neck.

To release, tori comes up to a crouching position, keeping pressure on uke's neck, and executes a forward roll over uke's head, coming to both feet and turning to face uke in a good defensive posture. Note that throughout the technique, tori's body is positioned as close as possible to uke's, uke's hips are squeezed with both knees, and tori's lower legs and feet are nearly under uke's thighs. This reduces the possibility that uke will have sufficient leverage to roll tori off before the choke is applied. This technique is designed to restrict the flow of blood to uke's brain, thus rendering the opponent unconscious.

a

b

c

Several systems of jujitsu distinguish between choking and strangling. *Choking* constricts blood flow to the brain and renders uke unconscious. *Strangling* restricts air flow to uke's lungs and will also render uke unconscious. If a choke is executed quickly and precisely, it can go unnoticed by uke until it's too late, whereas a stranglehold is usually painful and takes greater time to render the victim unconscious. Because strangles are painful, uke will struggle and fight harder. However, strangling can cause a great deal of damage to the cartilage in uke's neck, and if a stranglehold is executed properly, it can be devastating.

Many jujitsu systems make no distinction between the two, exchanging the terms randomly. This has the advantage of not confusing the jujitsuka with anything other than constricting the neck as quickly as possible. And in a real combat, one may not have the time to make the distinction. However, being able to execute both effectively gives the jujitsuka a greater range of options and can be tactically advantageous. If the object is to subdue the opponent, without causing lasting harm, then the choke is preferable, but the jujitsuka must practice earnestly in order to gain the skill to do so.

SELF-DEFENSE TIPS

- Be aware of your surroundings. Many shime techniques are more effective when pressing the opponent's body against an object or a wall.
- Be aware if there are multiple opponents. If you use shime, you must apply it swiftly.
- Use rolls to get away from your opponent and quickly regain your upright stance.
- Recognize that some shime arts work well without going to the ground.
- Strikes can be used on the ground to make shime more effective and to create opportunities to use the techniques.

REAR HOLD

In *ushiro gatame,* or a rear hold, uke punches at tori's face with the right hand. Tori ducks down slightly to the left while executing a passing block with the left hand. At the same time tori steps forward on the right foot and drives the right arm forward under uke's right arm and grabs high up on uke's right collar, palm up and fingers underneath the collar. Retaining a firm grip on uke's collar, tori rolls the right hand toward him- or herself while dropping the right elbow and steps back on the right foot, drawing uke off balance and pulling uke back. Uke and tori are now facing the same direction, uke's back against tori's chest.

Tori then reaches under uke's left arm with the left arm and attains a similar grip high up on uke's left lapel. This gives tori a hold known as the *full nelson* in western wrestling styles. Tori's hips are then thrust forward, breaking uke's balance and stance, and tori immediately sits down on the ground, pulling uke down between the legs. Tori then wraps both legs around to the inside of uke's legs, immobilizing uke's lower body, and continues to apply the full nelson hold. To release, tori holds tightly to uke, first rolling partially to the left to gain momentum; then tori suddenly rolls all the way to the right until uke is facedown to the ground, tori atop uke. Keeping pressure downward on uke's neck, tori disentangles both arms and executes a forward roll over uke's head. Tori comes to both feet, turns, and faces uke in a good defensive stance. Note that the full nelson part of this technique is often executed to apply severe pain to uke's neck by bending it forward. But properly executed it is a double-shoulder dislocation, and the pressure to the neck is an optional execution.

a

b

c

d

e

f

g

This is only a representative sampling of shime techniques. And for each technique there are several variations. Tactically, shime techniques are used as finishing techniques; but the more complex ones, such as *ushiro gatame,* presuppose that there is only one opponent or that any other opponents have already been defeated.

As jujitsuka gain skill in execution, they will be able to perform these shime techniques more swiftly and precisely. The simplest and most direct ones may then be used as devastating finishes in the presence of perhaps two or three opponents. But this is a judgment call to be made as the situation dictates.

At this point, we have looked at the component techniques used in most jujitsu systems. In the next chapter we explore assembling these techniques into a sequence.

CHAPTER

COMBINATIONS

n the previous chapters you have read a sampling of the basic technique categories common to most jujitsu styles. There are many more techniques in each category, as well as variations on those, giving rise to hundreds of combinations. At some point in the jujitsuka's development, there arises a need for training to join techniques together into a flow or sequence. One of the greatest strengths of jujitsu is the ability it affords its practitioners to flow from technique to technique, thus giving the opponent little or no time to react. Remember that a jujitsuka tries not to oppose strength with strength—nor box a boxer or wrestle a wrestler. When jujitsuka meet resistance, they flow past the resistance and turn it to their own advantage.

Remember, too, that some styles teach sequences of techniques as a whole from the beginning. Others teach the basic components first, only later beginning to join them together. There are merits to each approach, but by acquiring component parts first, a jujitsuka learns to extract precision from each move and thereby to enhance the effectiveness.

Some techniques work well against most opponents, but not against all. A simple leverage pry from a wrist or hand grip is a good example. If precise movements are followed and leverage maximized, this sort of escape works most of the time. But say your opponent finishes cement for a living or is a lumberjack who chops wood all day: the prying might not work against the incredible strength these individuals have in their hands. Therefore, the jujitsuka learns other techniques and how to flow right into a different move that will work. Sequences must be practiced to learn how to make techniques flow together.

These sequences also become credible self-defense sets that in themselves can be effective. Throughout this sort of sequential training the jujitsuka develops a feel for which moves will best set up the next technique. As an example, consider that you wish to set up a forward hip throw; a strike that sends your opponent reeling backward would in that case only make the throw more difficult. Several options, however, are available. You could deliver a strike that simply stuns the opponent or brings the opponent forward. You could take advantage of the strike and throw a different nage, one designed to take your opponent backward, or you could learn to execute the forward hip throw from behind the opponent. Jujitsuka must train to adapt themselves to changes in a situation, and to acquire that flexibility they must first have a large repertoire of techniques. Then they must train to execute the various techniques together, to "flow" into a sequence.

COMBINATION DEFENSES

This chapter contains a series of sequence sets, as well as a series of basic responses to standard self-defense situations. The sensei trains jujitsuka so that they may one day react spontaneously to almost any situation. Any serious practitioner of jujitsu can tell you of the magical day when he or she first unleashed a series of techniques against an attack in a way the jujitsuka had never executed before. It often happens so quickly and easily that the jujitsuka can hardly believe that it occurred. Often the jujitsuka will then try to re-create this sequence, only to find that he or she can't. That is because the jujitsuka reacted spontaneously, out of the muscle memory achieved through hundreds and hundreds of practice hours. And that is precisely what a jujitsuka hopes to achieve through training. That is the state that the sensei hopes to induce within each student.

Noted jujitsu master Henry Okazaki has said,

> Only by cultivating a receptive state of mind, without preconceived ideas or thoughts, can one master the secret art of reacting spontaneously and naturally without hesitation and without purposeless resistance.

SELF-DEFENSE TIPS

COMBINATIONS

1. Pay attention to your surroundings.

2. Imagine how you would deal with any type of attack in a variety of settings; use the power of visualization.

3. Know your strengths but also your limitations. Apply these to your visualizations.

4. Do not let your ego become an issue in a self-defense situation. Your emotions should not rule your response; remain detached.

5. Recognize potentially dangerous situations and seek to defuse or avoid them.

6. When faced with an actual self-defense situation, first determine how many opponents you face. Then develop your strategy accordingly.

7. When an actual situation occurs, do what is necessary to neutralize it. Then seek immediately to get additional help.

8. Good self-defense is about developing awareness. Practice techniques that accomplish this. As a martial artist you have nothing to prove, so if possible don't allow dangerous situations to develop. When they can't be avoided, however, apply all of your training to neutralizing the situation. Firmly set your intent to succeed.

MOUNTAIN STORM

This technique in its entirety is called *yama arashi* (mountain storm), and the name gives the feel of an entire mountain coming down upon the attacker. Uke attacks tori by striking with a right-handed hook punch to the face. Tori steps forward on the left foot and executes a cutting block (*shuto uke*) to the inside of uke's right wrist. Continuing to move, tori steps forward on the right foot and strikes uke's collarbone with a right-blade hand. The right-blade hand strike is the same movement as shuto uke but applied instead as a strike. Tori's right leg never stops, though, and continues past uke's right hip, slightly rising. Tori then forcefully reaps his or her right leg backward, calf to calf, and bends at the waist, thus throwing *osoto gari* (leg-reaping throw).

Tori retains control of uke's right arm with the left hand and of uke's collarbone with the right hand. This reaps uke off both feet to land forcefully on the back. Simultaneously, tori drops to both knees next to uke, barring uke's right arm over the right thigh and then reaching for uke's throat with the right hand. This will both strangle uke and bar uke's right elbow.

To release, tori puts downward pressure on uke's throat, comes to a crouch, executes a forward roll over uke's right shoulder, pivots, and then faces uke in a good defensive posture. This response set or sequence includes blocking (uke), striking (atemi), throwing (nage), incapacitating (shime), and rolling (kaiten).

a

b

c

d

e

HAND-NECK-FIST ENTANGLEMENT

The next technique is called *tekubi shigarami* (hand-neck-fist entanglement). Uke attacks tori with a straight, right punch to the face. Tori steps to uke's right side on the left foot while executing a right-handed passing block or parry. Then tori grabs uke's right wrist with the right hand, turns sharply to the right, strikes uke in the jaw with a left-handed, open-palm strike, and brings his or her left hand over and under uke's right arm to attain an entanglement on uke's right arm.

Tori next pivots 180 degrees counterclockwise, bringing uke's right arm in an arc that throws uke to the ground. Tori sits close to uke as uke falls, brings both knees up, slides the right hand up to cover the back of uke's hand, and administers a painful wristlock. Tori can choose to either use this hold as a painful submission or break uke's wrist. To release, tori bars uke's right arm against the right shin, levers uke to the right, and turns to the right in the same movement. Tori then stands up and assumes a good defensive posture. This sequence includes blocking (uke), striking (atemi), entanglement (shigarami), and joint locking (yawara).

a

b

c

d

e

f

NAKED STRANGLE

The following technique is called *hadaka jime* (naked strangle). Uke again attacks tori with a right-handed, straight punch to tori's face. Tori executes a right-handed passing block or parry and steps forward on the right foot. As tori pivots to the right, a left-handed palm strike is delivered to the back of uke's head, and tori ends up directly behind uke. Tori's left arm encircles uke's neck, and joins both hands together directly in front of uke's throat. As tori pulls both hands back against uke's throat, tori's forehead is placed against the back of uke's neck and drives forward. Here tori can strangle uke into submission or crush the throat.

To release, tori simply steps back while pulling uke rearward to the ground and assumes a good defensive posture. This technique employs a block (nagashi uke), a strike (palm strike), a strangle (hadaka jime), and a throw (ushiro nage).

a

b

c

d

SELF-DEFENSE RESPONSES TO COMMON ATTACKS

A common self-defense situation occurs when an attacker comes up behind the victim and traps both of the victim's arms in a bear hug from the rear. For example, uke gains a rear bear hug on tori. Tori reacts immediately by stomping downward on uke's right foot with the right heel. Uke is slightly distracted or hurt, and tori drops into a low, squatting stance; simultaneously tori points both hands forward and down and thrusts both arms forward as he rolls both shoulders inward. Tori then grabs uke's right arm with both hands near uke's shoulder, turns slightly to the left, drops to the right knee, and executes a right-shoulder throw. Uke lands on the back, and tori strikes to uke's throat with a right, knife-edge strike. Tori then releases uke and steps back into a good defensive stance.

a

b

c

d

e

WEAPON DEFENSES

Jujitsuka also practice defenses against attackers with weapons. Some styles begin this practice almost from the start of training. Others hold that weapon defenses should only be practiced after a basic level of skill has been achieved; the premise is that defense against weaponry requires a higher intensity of concentration and seriousness than is usually present at an early stage of jujitsu training. Defenses against armed opponents are essentially simple, but they must be executed as if one's life depended on their success. This requires great concentration and an attitude to succeed at all costs. Keep in mind that weapons defenses are far from perfect, especially when facing a skilled opponent. Always practice weapons defenses under the supervision of the sensei.

KNIFE DEFENSE

Uke attacks tori with a right-handed, straightforward knife thrust to the belly. Tori executes a tight, clockwise pivot but does not move off the position. Instead, as tori pivots, the hips drop back, shifting the weight to the left foot, thereby moving the midsection from the path of the knife. At the same time, tori's right arm executes a parry, while the left arm comes up to guard and block against uke's switching direction. Immediately, tori's right hand grasps uke's right hand—in order to control not only the hand but also the knife that it is holding. Tori's left hand lays against uke's right elbow and tori steps forward, barring uke's right arm, and executes a forearm takedown. Tori drops the left knee to the nerve above uke's right elbow. This frees tori's left hand and allows tori to secure uke's knife. Tori may elect to break or hyperextend uke's arm. Tori then steps back into a good defensive posture.

a

b

C

GUN DEFENSE

In the gun defense, uke is holding a gun against tori's chest with the right hand. Tori's hands are held up. In one motion, tori pivots tightly to the right (as in the knife defense), drops the left hand down to grasp uke's right hand, and secures the weapon. Tori then brings the right hand up to grasp uke's right hand and weapon; then tori pivots to the left and executes a wristlock to uke's right wrist. Uke will land on the back. Tori steps out on the left foot, stretching uke's right arm out, and then bars uke's right elbow against the right shin. This should cause uke to release the gun, if the wristlock didn't already, and allow tori to secure it. Tori then throws uke's right arm back across uke's body and steps back into a good defensive posture. Realize that tori has the option to severely strain or break uke's right wrist and elbow during the execution of this defense.

a

b

c

TECHNIQUE TIPS

1. Remember the goal in a defense against weapons is to gain control of the weapon.

2. Gaining control of the weapon usually requires controlling the hand that holds it.

3. When defending against a knife, know that you will get cut. Expect it.

4. Identify vital targets such as arteries—don't allow them to be easy targets.

5. Simple weapon defenses are usually the best and most effective.

6. Once you acquire some skill in weapon defenses, practice them with serious intent.

7. Learn to apply strikes and kicks in weapon defenses, but not at the expense of control.

8. Practice to make a given defense effective.

9. Then practice free play to gain control of the weapon, regardless of whether the defense works.

10. When practicing weapons defenses, have someone observe you closely. Students frequently get "cut" or "shot" when practicing, without even realizing that it happens. Strive for precision.

Weapon defenses can be very fancy, incorporating several strikes and moves. However, we omitted these from the sequences here for two reasons. First, jujitsuka practice weapon defenses with a slightly different mind-set than they have for other techniques. The object here is to secure the weapon as quickly as possible. This means movement and flow are maximally streamlined to attain this goal. If the opportunity for a strike presents itself, the jujitsuka may elect to take it, but the goal is to secure the weapon.

The second reason is that it takes several years of practice to be able to react spontaneously to openings for strikes. It is important in training to reinforce the concepts that securing the weapon is the goal and concentrating on the most simple and effective techniques best serves this purpose while minimizing the possibility of being injured from the weapon.

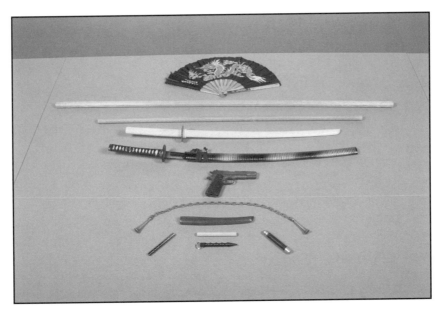

Weapons commonly used in jujitsu

Aside from working with the weapons commonly defended against (i.e., knives and guns), many jujitsu dojos use other traditional weapons. Some of these are the *yawara* stick, the *manriki gusari*, the *jo*, the *bo*, the *katana,* and the *bokken*. The yawara stick is a short stick or rod that is used to strike, apply nerve holds, and enhance leveraged moves. The manriki gusari is a weighted chain that can capture other weapons—as well as limbs—and choke or strangle. The bo and jo are larger sizes of sticks used for blocking and striking; they can also be used to throw an opponent. The katana is the sword used by the samurai and designed to cut or slice an opponent. The bokken is a wooden practice katana, but it can be used as a weapon to beat or smash an opponent. The tessan (iron fan) was carried by many samurai and was iron on the outside. Many high ranking bushi (military class/soldiers) as well as the emperor would forbid carrying weapons when they held audience. However, the tessan could be carried and provided a means of defense against edged weapons should treachery occur. The tessan can be used to strike, deflect knife or sword, and to obscure an opponent's vision.

The yawara stick

The manriki gusari

The jo

The bo

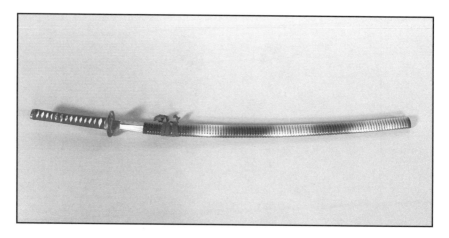

The katana

The bokken

The tessan

We have not shown the myriad of drills devised by sensei to instill in the jujitsuka a concept of flow. Putting techniques together in sequence is more than practicing techniques such as the ones shown here. It is also drilling—yes, over and over again—with different partners of various sizes, strengths, and temperaments to allow the jujitsuka to subconsciously process the way in which attackers might respond. This allows the jujitsuka to acquire the state of spontaneous flow.

Remember that various jujitsu styles approach the concepts of flow and sequencing differently and that there are pros and cons to each. But all require students to practice endlessly. Be cautious of styles that emphasize fancy, elaborate moves. In the end, simple is usually the most effective. As Henry Okazaki once said, "Acquiring the receptive state of mind does not come in 10 easy lessons."

CHAPTER

10

STRATEGIES
AND TACTICS

Throughout this book we have emphasized that practice is paramount. Few people have acquired skill in *any* activity without practice. Consider beginning jujitsuka, who have no experience at all with martial arts. Use of the mind has to become disciplined and focused. Concentration is an absolute must. Almost every activity and skill to be mastered involves movements and concepts that, at least at the surface, run counter to everything they have previously learned. Skills such as falling aren't necessary in day-to-day living. Abandoning oneself and letting go are alien and strange to most people. Staying relaxed, especially during times of stress or danger, is particularly difficult (think of our everyday accumulation of stress). Most beginning jujitsuka bring bad habits to the table, and they must slowly and methodically learn to change those habits to become proficient at jujitsu. The point is that all this requires practice, a great deal of practice, and if prospective students are resistant to being open, they will most likely never acquire the necessary skill to move forward.

In Japan's feudal era, practitioners were available for training daily, usually for many hours. Granted this was their chosen life path and profession—and in a context of life or death. Today, one would be hard-pressed to find a school or dojo that allowed a student to train every day of the week.

Most schools operate on a training regimen of two to three days per week. This is especially true for commercial schools that enroll students for specified and limited amounts of access or practice. This may be true only until a student attains a relative degree of skill; the sensei may then grant the student access to additional and more advanced training. Universities, park districts, and YMCAs and YWCAs may offer more practice time, but the truth is that budgets and available time can be arbitrary yet real governors of the time available for practice.

Whatever time is available, make the most of it. Stay for every available iota of practice time. Learn quickly to leave other considerations outside the dojo or off the mat. Open your mind like an empty vessel so that you may receive as much learning and information as possible. Know that the lessons you can hardly remember consciously nevertheless will remain within your subconscious if your intent is to learn. Any good sensei will tell you that four to six hours spent with an open mind and willingness to learn is worth twice as much time spent with poor concentration or resistant attitudes.

There are things that can help you to learn more thoroughly, however, if not more quickly. Read about jujitsu. Study its history and the many styles that are out there. Review books and tapes. Attend demonstrations of jujitsu and any other martial arts that you can. Find time to discuss your thoughts and feelings with other martial artists and other jujitsuka. Keep an up-to-date notebook of all that you learn. Review it frequently. Revise it as often as you feel necessary. Record within in it your observations about your lessons, as well as any thoughts you may have about martial arts in general.

Visualize your techniques as much as you can. See yourself executing techniques correctly and efficiently. Learn to see yourself succeeding. Present yourself as a willing uke for your sensei and senior students. You can learn much by receiving an art from a more skilled technician. And, finally, there will come a time when the sensei will begin to let you teach students more junior to you. Jump at this chance. You're likely to feel like a fool or be embarrassed more times than you'd care to think about, but this state will pass. What you learn through teaching cannot be taught to you. It can only be experienced.

KNOW THE SELF

Recognize that you are likely to experience all sorts of fears in your study of jujitsu. That is OK. Fears are often the expression of limitations we have imposed on ourselves. To overcome these limitations, it is necessary to walk through these fears. Take falling as an example. Nearly all of us have an abiding fear of falling down. That is why we reach for the ground when it happens, trying to prevent injury. That is also how we tend to get hurt.

Training in jujitsu is designed to let you gradually work through your fears. Falling is *taught* in stages, each one a bit more potentially dangerous than the last. As students gain skill in one stage, they are pressed to the next. The sensei's art is to get students to move through their fears without even realizing that they are doing so. Eventually students notice they are able to fall, and what seemed impossible a short time before is no longer a fiction.

The feeling of accomplishment is extraordinary. The sensei lets students realize this—and then moves them on to yet a more challenging and dangerous activity. Eventually students believe that they can indeed overcome their fears; they begin to recognize the need to pass through them and are no longer afraid to try. They come to believe in themselves, and their training accelerates.

Fears come in many guises. Fear of failure is one of the greatest. Make no mistake; you will fail. You will fail a great many times. Think of these occasions not as failures but as practices for success. You will go home disappointed, disgusted, angry, or full of self-doubt. Of course, this happens to us in everyday life as well. By returning to practice, however, you provide yourself with the opportunity to work through all these negative emotions and to ultimately succeed. This success often transfers itself beyond jujitsu and self-defense encounters.

Emotions are very much a part of a jujitsuka's life, and an accomplished master is one who has come to grips with personal emotions, not banished them. In combative struggles, emotions can be deadly. Yet one cannot banish them completely. So one must learn to control and then detach from them. This can only be done through experience; know that it will take time to succeed.

Know that by believing in yourself, you will persevere and progress. Understand that each of us carries individual baggage; we can't measure progress accurately by how fast *others* are progressing. They carry baggage, too, and probably they find themselves measuring their progress against yours. In the end, it all evens out: envy and pride get you nowhere. You can take pride in your accomplishments, but recognize that greater hurdles to overcome will always exist. In this realization you may begin to understand humility.

Humility sets the stage for an open and questing mind. And as you open your mind, your ability to learn and succeed accelerates.

In order to succeed, set your intent to do so. Talk about this to your sensei. Likely the sensei will make time to share his or her thoughts with you. Perhaps the sensei will share his or her own experiences in this regard. Listen closely. Learn from others' experiences, but realize that the only profound learning is experiential. How else will you yourself have experiences to share one day?

CULTIVATE THE SELF

Any book on martial arts is likely to state that one of the benefits of martial arts training is coordination of the mind and body. Day-to-day living seems to do little to enhance this coordination. Many people engage in little or no physical activity. When they do undertake such activity, it is usually to get in shape, lose weight, socialize, have fun, or reduce stress. Most activities don't truly stress coordination of the mind and body. Regular and disciplined practice with particular goals in mind is required to effect this mind-body coordination. In jujitsu such coordination begins with encountering, recognizing, owning, and then working through one's fears and self-imposed limitations.

CLEARING YOUR MIND

In a regular practice session within a dojo, the sensei constantly reminds students, by word and example, to keep their minds on what they are doing. The sensei usually seeks to limit distractions so that students attend to their practice, but at some point will require them to practice with all manner of distractions in order to test and stretch the limits of their concentration. Cultivating an open mind, the students become empty vessels, ready to receive lessons and input; the foundations of humility are laid down. This prepares students for a true combative situation, where the gleaning of the slightest input or nuance may make the difference.

As jujitsuka progress through their training, they come to realize that the slightest shift in weight, posture, or placement of hands will make the difference in a technique's being effective or ineffective. In other words, they must pay attention to the body. Gradually jujitsuka begin to accumulate a sense about the proper use of the body. After a great deal of practice this body sense becomes second nature—which can occur only if the mind and body become synchronized. And this must be preceded by a *clearing* of the mind, a *letting go* of the internal dialogue. Jujitsuka are directed to leave all of their everyday concerns at the edge of the *tatami* (mat). That's easy enough to say—but not so easy to do. But by focusing attention on practice, it follows that the internal dialogue soon is only about the object of attention, that is, practice. Eventually, as students acquire a new body sense, they learn that even the internal dialogue about practice must cease in order for them to act without hesitation and preconceived notions.

UNFOCUSED VISION

There are several activities that students may practice to reinforce these lessons, and they need not be limited to time spent in the dojo. Jujitsuka are taught, for example, that when facing an opponent, they should not let their vision be drawn to just one thing but should take in everything. If jujitsuka focus on the oncoming fist, they are likely to not see the *other* fist. So they are taught to use unfocused vision. In this way they are able to process all the visual cues and input within the perceptual field.

It is often said, both within and without martial arts, to watch the eyes of your opponent because the eyes tell all. Yet if the opponent is practiced in using the eyes to draw your attention in a particular direction, then you will be set up for a potentially devastating attack. Therefore, students in the dojo learn to see everything, without focusing on one thing in particular.

Outside the dojo, students are encouraged to sit in any given setting and then try to focus on only one sight, one sound, or one feeling. They will eventually be able to see or hear or feel the one thing to the exclusion of all else. Then they will practice opening their perceptions to see everything in the perceptual field, making no distinctions among whatever is present.

Try to walk sometime without concentrating on anything in particular. This can be difficult at first, but eventually you will succeed, and it will change the way you move through the world. Our world is overloaded with input. As we grow, we learn to filter out most of these distractions in order to go about our business. This is generally well and good, but it can rob us of valuable information. This screening of input eventually becomes habit, and it can be self-limiting though it seems necessary for survival. A sight-impaired person quickly learns to process information other than visual. Try blindfolding yourself and moving about a room; you quickly begin to attend to other cues.

By practicing to focus attention on one thing purposefully, you will build concentration. By opening to all input, you will still your mind. By practicing both of these mind-sets you can attain a flexible and present state of mind. This is a powerful enhancement to your ability to do jujitsu.

BREATHING

Correct breathing is yet another aspect of mind-body coordination. Proper breathing will allow jujitsuka to maximize everything they do. Training in breathing begins when jujitsuka learn to fall. To allow the body to absorb the shock of a fall, students learn to exhale. This seems to run against what anyone does naturally: most people hold their breath when they begin to fall. But this is very punishing to the body. As you inhale and hold your breath, you automatically tense your body. When you exhale, in contrast, your musculature relaxes. You then freely allow the shock of falling to be absorbed by the body and the mat.

As jujitsuka progress to the other techniques, they begin to see that all movement is enhanced through exhaling. This becomes readily apparent as jujitsuka begin to learn nage. Throwing is clumsy and ineffective if one inhales during the *kake* (execution). But by exhaling, the movement is accomplished with smoothness and power.

Karate and other striking arts utilize the power gained by exhaling as one strikes, and their practitioners train accordingly. Specialized breathing techniques are introduced to karate students to teach them how to focus and concentrate their power. While jujitsuka don't necessarily incorporate all such techniques, breathing *correctly* is integral to the effective execution of jujitsu techniques. Most oriental fighting systems teach that proper breathing allows one to accumulate, focus, and ultimately deliver the *chi* (the body's innate energy) to any technique.

HEALING ARTS

Healing arts are yet another aspect of the most developed jujitsu systems. Most oriental fighting systems incorporate aspects of oriental philosophy. Fundamental to this philosophy is the concept of *yin* and *yang*. Yin and yang speak to the fact that all things exist in regard to their polar opposites: light and dark, cold and hot, male and female, active and passive. Within yang there is yin; within yin there is yang. Fighting is by nature yang; healing is by nature yin. So healing can be seen as the yin aspect of jujitsu.

Traditionally, healing arts were an integral part of jujitsu. In a combative environment, the ability to heal injuries effectively gave the parent system a great advantage. These arts were so important that they were often among the most closely guarded secrets of a system, which might explain why so few systems teach them today. In more modern systems, healing arts are incorporated to deal primarily with training injuries. However, the deeper jujitsu systems teach techniques that deal not only with training injuries but with the more traditional arts of restoration and resuscitation from life-threatening injures and techniques.

Traditional healing arts were based on the precepts of traditional Oriental medicine (TOM) and folk medicine. TOM maintains that bodily health depends on the proper ebb and flow of chi. All aspects of the body exist in a balance, and all things are related to each other. Treatment of injuries addresses not only mechanical aspects but also the innate energetics. Jujitsuka should seek to become knowledgeable in the concepts of TOM and chi for two reasons: First, understanding TOM allows students to see the relationship of chi cultivation to enhancing their overall health and effectiveness as martial artists. Second, by understanding this relationship, they can more effectively cope with the injuries they and others incur and also set the stage for their training in the more esoteric aspects of jujitsu.

Today's "I'm not at fault; you are" environment mandates that sensei make use of western medical solutions to traumatic injury as well. The most complete jujitsu systems require their sensei to be qualified in first aid and CPR. But they still require their sensei to be fundamentally skilled in the application of traditional healing techniques. By requiring their sensei to be skilled, knowledgeable, and certified in both Eastern and Western healing arts, they ensure the safety of their students. Knowledge of anatomy and physiology, herbal liniments, and rehabilitation as well as skill in kappo, katsu, athletic taping, and massage deepen the jujitsuka's understanding and practice of this most profound martial art.

Meditation is another way to practice the cultivation of chi as well as proper breathing and mind-body coordination. Religious and various belief systems (as well as fighting arts) in Asia stress the importance of meditation. Meditation reduces stress physiologically, relaxes the mind and body, and lowers blood pressure. In addition it clears the mind, enhances the flow of chi, and centers the individual. There are far too many methods of meditation to enumerate them all here. The most powerful ones focus on breathing correctly, primarily by breathing with the diaphragm.

Many systems teach seated, or still, meditation. *Tai chi*, a Chinese martial art and system of health enhancement, has been called moving meditation. The movements—slow and totally coordinated with the breathing—ultimately allow practitioners to accomplish amazing feats. It is the meditative and coordinated breathing aspects that make tai chi one of the most powerful combat systems in the world. *Chi gung* is the practice of specific movement and breathing sets, which allow practitioners to accumulate and circulate chi in specific ways to enhance their health as well as fighting ability.

Almost all jujitsu systems teach some form of meditation. What may vary among the systems is when they introduce students to meditation. Some systems teach meditation from the outset of training; others wait until students acquire basic combat skills. Regardless of when the meditation method is introduced, its importance to jujitsu cannot be overstressed. The benefits to both the mind and body allow jujitsuka to greatly enhance their skills. Ultimately, the practice of meditation leads jujitsuka to a state of mind called *mu shin*, a state of "no mind." This is the state of mind that jujitsuka wish to maintain in combat. This is what allows jujitsuka to respond spontaneously and without preconceived notions.

Meditation is a great way to strengthen the mind *and* body.

FIGHTING TACTICS

There is a wide variation in what individual jujitsu styles and instructors choose to emphasize among tactics. What constitutes tactics for a beginner or an experienced practitioner varies as well. Jujitsu is largely regarded as defensive in nature, and for many styles defense is the emphasis for students in their first few years of training. According to an old belief, students below brown-belt level know just enough to get themselves in trouble. At brown-belt level, they begin to use techniques with efficiency and power, but still lack sufficient control. At black-belt level they begin to acquire the control, effectiveness, and power to reach the devastating potential the techniques were intended to deliver. It is at this point that jujitsu can take on a decidedly offensive nature.

Some styles go straight to teaching jujitsu as an offensive art. This is not necessarily wrong. But one of the strengths of this martial art is that it enables a wide range of responses to almost any situation. Teaching jujitsu from a defensive point of view would seem to enhance an individual's ability to use a wide range of responses, much as a law-enforcement official uses gradually escalating force to meet greater threat. Teaching jujitsu strictly from an offensive point of view can make it difficult for a jujitsuka to learn to scale down the response to a less dangerous threat.

DISTANCING

To understand tactics at all requires a basic understanding of *ma ai* (distancing). Each martial art has an optimum distance within which its techniques are most effective. Karate, for instance, must allow for strikes and kicks to attain their greatest amount of power (and, thus, effectiveness). For karate practitioners the most effective ma ai is somewhere between arm and leg's length. Jujitsu is most effective close into the opponent, that is, within throwing and grabbing distance. Correct ma ai for the jujitsuka is right next to the opponent.

From the viewpoint of tactics, jujitsu executed from a defensive point of view requires letting the opponent get in close to you. Fighting is generally regarded by most martial arts as nonproductive and to be avoided. Jujitsuka seek to spot a developing situation and try to avoid or defuse it. When this can't be done, jujitsuka will often let the opponent make the first move and then respond as the situation dictates. Letting the opponent within the proper ma ai allows jujitsuka to be most effective.

Once an attack is initiated, jujitsuka then blend with it and turn the attack to their advantage. Attackers are rapidly taken to the ground in most cases, as few antagonists are comfortable with ground fighting. The strength of response is guided by the situation's circumstances. Neutralizing an attack from an obnoxious drunk, for example, rarely merits as firm a response as does an attack from a knife-wielding opponent. Both merit a decisive response, but the drunk's attack is usually more a matter of the jujitsuka's controlling and distancing, while handling the knife-wielder must include the intent to defeat. Some concepts are fundamental to good defense: for example, maintaining a high degree of awareness, positioning to minimize the number of directions of an attack, and keeping an eye open for multiple attackers. In fact, these concepts are fundamental to both good defense and offense, and they should rapidly become habits that jujitsuka maintain throughout everyday life.

GAINING THE UPPER HAND

Good offense is all about seeing the attack before it happens and neutralizing it as rapidly as possible. In the offense, jujitsuka bring to bear all their knowledge gained through training. This includes being aware of all the mistakes made through their training, such as poor stance work, poor balance, weak defensive postures, and poor follow-through. Jujitsuka look for these characteristics and others in the attacker. When they observe them, jujitsuka exploit these mistakes on the part of the attacker and deliver a devastating attack to take advantage of them. Jujitsuka look to move rapidly, presenting opponents with little or no opportunity to acquire a target, seeking by the sheer quickness and flexibility of their offense to give the attacker no chance to mount an effective attack.

Offense is delivered with a focused intent and fierceness that enables the jujitsuka to immediately gain the upper hand. Strategies may be based on moving against the attacker's centerline, the attacker's dead angles (corners), or going high or low depending on the attacker's fighting style.

Offense often begins with a movement designed to draw the opponent's attention away from the main offensive thrust. For instance, a low, quick painful kick may draw the opponent's attention downward while the main offense is actually executed higher up. Higher-level arts in jujitsu often teach ways in which to distract an opponent's attention away from where the real technique will be applied. But unleashing offense from the jujitsuka is like "reaping the whirlwind." Given that most jujitsuka first learn to respond to threatening situations defensively, they are of a mind-set to execute restraint when applying techniques. But forced by circumstances to become offensive, jujitsuka become devastating in their flow and are trained to accept nothing but the utter defeat of the opponent. Make no mistake: the techniques of jujitsu can be gentle, painful, punishing, or crippling. When compelled to the offense, jujitsuka will often let dissolve the restraint that has characterized their defensive training.

This will occur, however, only if training in offensive fighting is introduced into the training curriculum. Understand that well-trained jujitsuka carry into combat a wide range of responses and techniques and are prepared to use them should the occasion arise.

In the beginning stage and for several years to follow, it seems that all students can manage is to train their bodies to effectively execute the complex and unusual movements that constitute jujitsu techniques. But even early on in their training, jujitsuka begin to confront their personal, emotional, and mental limitations, which have accumulated throughout their lives. They quickly recognize the need for methods of training the mind and emotions. By knowing the self, by developing tactics for personal success, and by practicing methods of personal cultivation, they can attend more closely to developing effective tactics for fighting. Much of jujitsu is not about just becoming a warrior, but becoming a complete warrior.

CHAPTER

11

COMPETITIONS

nterest in marital arts competitions is strong these days. Virtually any style of jujitsu has a means by which its students may compete. Most often these take the form of in-class activities that enhance training. Within any given dojo, competitions may be designed to accomplish particular training goals, which may vary according to style, sensei, and student population. A considerable number of jujitsu practitioners don't consider these activities to be competitions but are willing to entertain them as training drills.

Many sensei de-emphasize the concept of competition, holding to the belief that the greatest competition is always with the self. They further believe that competition can induce pride, which only enhances the ego; they encourage jujitsuka to lose their attachments to the ego if they want to reach their highest potential. Still other sensei believe that competition engenders a state of mind far different from that necessary to utterly defeat your opponent in any real combat or self-defense. If competition takes the form of testing and improving one's skills in the dojo, and the sensei seeks to de-emphasize pridefulness, then students can usually avoid the trap of too much ego enhancement.

There is a great deal of benefit to testing one's skills. Until recently, however, competition within jujitsu styles had been minimal, primarily, it would seem, to avoid the potential for injury. Given the wide variety of jujitsu techniques designed to cause injuries, the charged atmosphere of competition makes it difficult to maintain the control necessary to preclude injury while executing techniques. In other words, competition seems to encourage the expression of great strength to overcome the lack of technique.

Competitors often try to force a technique with strength, and there is only so much stress that joints of the body can take. A competitor who lacks sufficient control and has the adrenaline flowing may apply a technique beyond the point of safety and cause a serious injury before realizing he or she has done so. While the competitor may regret having caused serious injury to the opponent, the injured student will still have many weeks or months of recovery and rehabilitation ahead. Training injuries are likely to occur to some extent given the nature of a martial art, and any jujitsuka who has practiced for several years carries the reminders of such injuries throughout his or her life. In a charged competitive atmosphere, however, injuries may be more extensive than otherwise and occur much more frequently.

KATA

Several forms of competition nevertheless do exist in jujitsu. The kata competition requires that a competitor have a partner who may or may not be competing, and together they make up a team. Each team is required to perform a series of techniques matching its skill level. Several of the techniques are selected by the competition's organizers, and the team is required to select a smaller number of optional techniques. Then these techniques are performed by each individual team—at a safe speed. The competitors are judged on effectiveness, style, control, presentation, and focus. A range of points is assigned to each criterion, and each technique is judged and scored by a panel of senior practitioners, usually black belts. The team is then required to create a combat sequence utilizing all the techniques. The sequence is executed at a faster speed, and it is judged on realism, creativity, originality, flow, and effectiveness. Again, points are assigned to each criterion, and all points from the kata and combative sequences are totaled to attain the final score.

FREESTYLE

In a freestyle competition, the competitor is attacked in a rapid series by several designated opponents. The types of attacks may be designated ahead of time or left up to the attackers. The object is for the competitor to effectively neutralize the attack, defeat the opponent, and then turn to face the next attacker as quickly as possible. The competitor is judged on control, effectiveness, maintaining a calm demeanor, and having a variation of responses. Many competitors use the same techniques to respond to all attacks. To score highly, however, a competitor must vary the types of counters and techniques according to the attack presented. Points are assigned to the various criteria, but scoring can be a great deal more subjective than with the kata competition. Striking is usually expected in a freestyle competition, but not in the kata competition. Competitive classifications are usually based on rank and vary from system to system.

SHIAI

Many styles of jujitsu use the *shiai,* developed in judo as a means of competition. Judo shiai allows free application of most techniques in a full-speed match. One point *(ippon)* is the maximum any competitor may score. A competitor can score an *ippon* by cleanly and decisively throwing the opponent to the ground, thereby ending the match.

Matches begin with the opponents standing face to face in a clearly defined match area measuring 30 feet by 30 feet. Matches are officiated by one referee and two judges; they can last from 3 to 20 minutes. In addition, timekeepers are required. Throws that are not clean and decisive may be awarded half points *(waza ari)*. Two waza ari are sufficient to win a shiai "by decision" but cannot outscore a cleanly attained ippon.

Once on the ground, a competitor continually seeks to place the opponent in joint locks (elbows only), chokes, or entanglements, attempting to get the opponent to submit. Open-hand strangles are prohibited. Submission results in an automatic win despite the point totals. Competitors may be awarded partial points for attaining submission holds, but the referees have the option to separate the opponents if the submission techniques fail to fully succeed and then to return them to the starting stand-up position. Competitors may be penalized partial points if it is seen that they are stalling. Matches are timed, and if neither competitor attains an *ippon* or a submission, then the match is decided on the total points scored. There is no striking in shiai. Tournaments may be single or double elimination. National or regional tournaments are divided into senior and junior divisions.

SUBMISSION GRAPPLING

Submission grappling is yet another style of competition. In this style the opponents begin in an upright position and attempt to get each other to the ground. Unlike the shiai point system, no points at all are awarded. The object is to put opponents on the ground and apply chokes, strangles, arm and leg bars, joint locks, or entanglements to get them to submit. Matches have no time limit and may go on for quite a long time. Clearly, conditioning is critical to success in submission grappling. Throws tend to be minimized, and quick takedowns are the norm. There is no striking in submission grappling. Tournaments are single elimination, sometimes with a consolation round for third and fourth place. Match areas are usually regulation wrestling- or boxing-ring size.

EXTREME FIGHTING

Cage Matches, Ultimate Fighting, and Extreme Fighting are the most dangerous forms of competition. These competitions are touted as no-holds-barred. This is basically true. Although attacks to the eyes and groin are not permitted, everything else is. Throws, strikes, kicks, chokes, strangles, joint locks, entanglements, and any manner of techniques are permitted. The

JUDO SHIAI DIVISIONS

SENIOR DIVISION

- White belt—beginner to yonkyu
- Brown belt—sankyu, nikkyu, and ikkyu
- Black belt—shodan and above

OLYMPIC SENIORS

- 150 pounds and under
- 176 pounds and under
- Unlimited or heavy weight
- Open category; no weight consideration

JUNIOR DIVISION

- Eleven divisions; one for each year of age from 6 through 16

OLYMPIC JUNIORS

- Light midget—light half of the contestants 10 years and under
- Heavy midget—heavy half of the contestants 10 years and under
- Light juniors—light half of 11 and 12 year olds
- Heavy juniors—heavy half of 11 and 12 year olds
- Light intermediate—light half of 13 and 14 year olds
- Heavy intermediate—heavy half of 13 and 14 year olds
- Light seniors—light half of 15 and 16 year olds
- Heavy seniors—heavy half of 15 and 16 year olds

object is to defeat your opponent completely by knockout, choke out, or submission. Often a competitor wins by pummeling the opponent into submission. All techniques are executed at full speed and full power. There is no time limit to the matches. Losers tend to incur injuries, sometimes serious ones. Tournaments are single elimination with only one winner, and there is usually a cash prize for the winner. Match areas are usually the size of regulation boxing rings. This form of competition is the closest to real combat, but serious injuries may result (and, in a recent match, even death). Because of this, more rules have been incorporated.

We have described, in major detail only, the most common forms of competition entered by jujitsuka. To get a real sense of what it's all about, attend a competition. Competition can be a valuable training tool for any jujitsuka. Beyond sharpening skills, it serves to put jujitsuka in the position of having to react to situations without thinking. In addition, regular competition can improve the individual's conditioning. This is especially true in any sort of grappling or ground fighting.

Though the benefits of competition are many, there are also dangers. Injuries occur. And many students become focused on competition for its own sake, ignoring the many other aspects of their training. An obsession with competition may be ego-based.

When searching for a jujitsu style, try to become aware of the sensei's and the style's emphasis on competition. If you are deeply opposed to competitions, try to find a style that more closely matches your temperament. But don't throw out the baby with the bath water. Recognize that, even if you are opposed to competition, the sensei may see some need for or benefit to your exposure to it. When you find a good sensei, trust your sensei's judgment regarding your training and development.

CHAPTER

12

CONDITIONING

By now you should be aware of the rigors of jujitsu training. You can put more into—and will get more out of—jujitsu if you train hard and stay in condition.

The first year of training is usually the most challenging because you are learning how to fall. Falling can be uncomfortable until you learn to relax. In truth, tensing when you fall may result in bruises and muscle strains or spasms. However, after you learn to relax (which is a very important skill in life as in jujitsu), falls become routine and eventually automatic. Getting over this first hurdle is an accomplishment. Many students with fantasies of instant self-defense never learn how to fall and soon stop training. Some instructors have students practice prolonged falling to see if they have the drive to come back to class. Jujitsu is not given, it is earned. When you know that you can take a fall, you will have earned the privilege to continue your studies. In addition, your self-confidence will improve, you will become more assertive, and you will be able to enjoy the art more than ever.

As soon as you learn to fall, you will probably begin to learn to throw. In addition to the excitement of throwing and falling, you now must deal with a new tension: that of throwing and being thrown, not just of falling.

As you begin to learn to throw, you will often do it incorrectly and apply strength where proper positioning and good kuzushi (off-balancing) are required. You will ask your body to move and position itself in ways that it has never moved before. Proper warm-up and stretching are essential. As you begin to practice joint locks, reflexive tensing may result in strains and sprains to the tendons and ligaments. Again, relaxation, thorough warm-ups, and stretching are keys to injury prevention. Once you stay relaxed as a general state of being, aches and pains will become fewer and less serious.

There is a great paradox about conditioning for jujitsu. When techniques are executed properly, with attention to proper breathing, relaxation, correct positioning, good leverage, and superior mind-body coordination, it becomes apparent that extensive conditioning isn't necessary. Many experienced jujitsuka have observed sensei who do no warm-up other than a mental one, or they have seen sensei with severe disabilities perform the most elegant and effective jujitsu. To get to this level, however, you must train hard for a great many years. Jujitsuka who compete in judo or submission grappling are likely to embark on a much more rigorous conditioning program that especially includes aerobic conditioning.

STRETCHING

Stretching is perhaps the most important aspect of conditioning for jujitsu. Considering the wide range of body motions and movements that the jujitsuka must learn, flexibility will greatly reduce the potential for injury. Care must be taken to properly warm up the tissues of the body. This warm-up includes gradually stretching each of the major muscle groups to increase blood flow to the muscles and to release the tensions of the day. Most dojos will use standard exercises, such as shoulder shrugs, arm rotations, leg lifts, and waist turns, to prepare you for more rigorous activities. Remember that these activities are to just get your blood flowing, not to see who can do them the fastest or most powerfully.

Several texts explain stretching in far greater detail than we can here. You should consult one of these texts if you want a more detailed explanation of the mechanics and physiology of stretching. Basic considerations of proper stretching include the following:

TECHNIQUE TIPS

- Stretching is a slow and gradual process. Do not rush.
- Exhale as you stretch. Exhale from the start to the full range of the stretch.
- Do not bounce as you stretch; such "ballistic stretching" can cause injury. Make your motions smooth and gradual.
- Stretch as far as you comfortably can.
- To begin to lengthen the stretch, do the movement a second time and it hold momentarily. Then push the stretch a bit farther.
- Give the stretched muscle group a moment to rest between stretches.
- If you feel a tearing, searing, or electric sensation, release the stretch immediately. These are signs of overstretching. Relax the muscle by shaking it and then massage it. If the sensation persists, notify the sensei. Likely the sensei will have you apply a balm or liniment or may have you ice it. Cease stretching that muscle group and avoid motions that may aggravate it.
- A re-stretching of the major muscle groups is recommended at the end of practice.

Stretches vary from class to class. Particular attention should be paid to the back, shoulders, wrists, fingers, legs, and neck. If you develop nagging problems, be sure to consult the sensei or senior students for some individual instruction. You may be stretching incorrectly. Remember that by stretching improperly, you may injure opposing muscle groups as well as tendons and ligaments. Once you begin to gain a greater degree of flexibility, you will feel great and will wonder why you haven't done this before. The following are examples of stretches for each of the areas requiring the most attention.

BACK STRETCH

Lying on your back, bring your knees to your chest and hold them in place with your arms. Muscle groups being stretched include the erector spinae, rhomboids, and quadratus lumborum.

SHOULDER STRETCH

Bring your right arm across the front of your body, holding it in place with your left arm. This movement stretches the rhomboids, deltoids, and teres major and minor. Repeat the exercise on your left arm.

WRIST STRETCH

Rotate your right hand, palm up. With your left hand reach under your right hand and grasp the base of your thumb. The right hand is then rotated outward, to the maximum extent. This rotation stretches the wrist flexors and extensors. Repeat the exercise on your left wrist.

FINGER STRETCH

Grab your right index finger with your left hand and bend it gradually backward. Repeat the stretch for each finger and thumb for both the left and right hands. This movement stretches the finger flexors, the wrist flexors, and the ligaments and tendons of the hand and wrist.

HAMSTRING STRETCH

Sit on the floor with your right leg extended forward and flat to the floor. Your foot can be held upright or relaxed. Bend forward at the waist as if to touch your nose to your toes. This stretch works the hamstrings and the various low back muscles. Go only so far as is comfortable and keep your back as straight as possible

NECK STRETCH

While facing forward, lean your head directly to the right, then to the front, and left holding the stretch at each position. Muscles stretched include the trapezius, scalenes, sternocleidomastoid, and levator scapulae.

When stretching, hold the stretch at the limit of your range of motion for three to five seconds. Release the stretch and repeat.

ENDURANCE

Endurance for jujitsu training is acquired by the continuous practice of the techniques. In the beginning, you will usually find yourself fatigued by the end of a practice. At first, you will be expending far more energy than necessary. By learning to relax and to synchronize breathing with movements, far less energy will be expended. Grappling and ground-fighting drills and competitions will also increase your endurance. Occasionally, a sensei will introduce some sort of speed drill, such as having you throw 10 throws as rapidly as possible. Finally, a good diet and plenty of rest are essential to building endurance.

STRENGTH

Despite the fact that good jujitsu relies more on momentum, timing, and leverage than on strength, you will build strength as you practice. Strength is developed intentionally through a variety of exercises, such as push-ups and sit-ups, and coincidentally through throwing and grappling. Incidentally, the concept of strength has another meaning in jujitsu. Remember that what we measure about strength is not "strength" but rather "resistance." That is, opponents do not have "200 pounds of strength" in their chest, arms, and shoulders; they have the ability to overcome 200 pounds of resistance. Hence, in jujitsu, you can deprive stronger opponents of their strength by not offering any resistance, by giving way without giving up or giving in.

PUSH-UPS

The following are several types of push-ups that strengthen the arms and shoulders, as well as other major muscle groups. When practicing push-ups, keep your arms close to your body and keep your back straight to maximize the resistance against which the targeted muscle groups work.

Hands flat on the floor

Using only the fingertips

Fingers pointed toward the feet

Using the outside edges of the hands

a

b

c

Three step push-up

ABDOMINAL EXERCISES

The following are abdominal strengthening exercises. When exercising the abdominal muscles be careful to maintain proper posture and body alignment to avoid undo stress on the back. In particular, do not curl your neck.

Crunches

Oblique crunches

Partner exercise

Oblique twists

PLYOMETRICS

Plyometric exercises are accomplished by execution of stance work for the legs and the rest of the body by the practice and execution of techniques. Leaping drills, such as the one pictured here, are also an example of plyometrics. These types of exercises increase speed and power. They also help create quicker reflexes for faster movements in attacking or defending.

STRIKING AND KICKING DRILLS

There are a myriad of striking and kicking drills that can be applied to improve these skills. Use of the heavy bag, kick shields, and hand targets is popular. While the emphasis in some drills is on speed and agility, in the early stages you should focus more on good body mechanics. Working against the heavy bag quickly reveals poor structural alignment and incorrect posture. Kick shields allow for the target to move, causing you to focus on quickly regaining good postural alignment before delivering the next strike or kick. In some classes, one student wears padding while another practices strikes on the padded student. At first this is a static process, but it becomes more of a challenge as the target student begins to move, changing postures and positions.

Kicking a kick shield

Striking focus mitts

Remember that conditioning should be a gradual and incremental process. A smaller number and duration of exercises and stretches done *well* yield far greater benefits than a greater number and duration of exercises done incorrectly.

A note about injuries. Most injuries in jujitsu fit into two categories: the overuse, overstretch, or overstrain of a muscle; and trauma, including bad falls, abrasions, and muscle or bone bruising from strikes or kicks. You must learn to train within your limits. Many students try to work through injuries to show courage and dedication. This attitude is fine, but constant aggravation of seemingly insignificant injuries can lead to chronic conditions that are difficult to correct. For this reason, always notify the sensei or senior students of any injury, no matter how small or insignificant.

Jujitsu conditioning focuses primarily on good warm-ups, good stretching, and attaining flexibility for any given muscle group undergoing a wide range of motion. Strength training comes from exercises such as push-ups and abdominal crunches and seeks to add greater resilience to withstand the many stresses that jujitsu training brings to the body, particularly to your joints. But primarily the best conditioning results from the repeated and regular practice of the techniques themselves. This steady practice, combined with attention to proper diet and sleep, will ensure your ability to participate in jujitsu for many years to come.

BIBLIOGRAPHY

Crowley, C., and B. Crowley. 1993. *Moving With The Wind: Magic and Healing in the Martial Arts.* St. Paul: Llewellyn Publications.

Draeger, D., and R. Smith. 1980. *Comprehensive Asian Fighting Arts.* Tokyo: Kodansha International, Ltd.

Draeger, D. *Classical Judo.* New York: John Weatherhill, Inc., 1973, p. 122

Funakoshi, G. 1973. *Karate-Do Kyohan: The master Text.* Tokyo/New York/San Francisco: Kodansha International, Ltd.

Hancock, H., and K. Higashi. 1961. *The Complete Kano Jiu-Jitsu (Judo).* New York: Dover Publications.

King, W. 1993. *Zen and the Way of the Sword: Arming the Samurai Psyche.* New York/Oxford: Oxford University Press.

Kirby, G. 1983. *Jujitsu: Basic Techniques of the Gentle Art.* Burbank, CA: Ohara Publications, Inc.

Kudo, K. 1967. *Dynamic Judo–Grappling Techniques.* San Francisco: Japan Publications Trading Company.

Kudo, K. 1967. *Dynamic Judo–Throwing Techniques.* San Francisco: Japan Publications Trading Company

Lie, F.T. 1988. *Tai Chi Chuan: The Chinese Way.* New York: Sterling Publishing, Co., Inc.

Mitchell, D. 1988. *The Overlook Martial Arts Handbook.* Woodstock, NY: The Overlook Press.

Mitose, J. 1981. *What Is Self-Defense? (Kenpo Jui-Jitsu).* Sacramento, CA: Kosho-Shorei Publishing Company.

Mushashi, M. 1974. Translated by V. Harris. *The Book of Five Rings.* Woodstock: The Overlook Press.

Nakae, K. 1958. *Jui Jitsu Complete.* Secaucus, NJ: Citadel Press.

Okazaki, H. 1929. *The Science of Self-Defense for Girls and Women.* Kahului, Maui: Henry Seishiro Okazaki.

Oyama, M. 1965. *This Is Karate.* Tokyo: Japan Publications Trading Co.

Random, M. 1978. *The Martial Arts.* London: Octopus Books, Ltd.

Ratti, O., and A. Westbrook. 1973. *Secrets of the Samurai.* Rutland: Charles E. Tuttle.

Tsunemoto, Y. (translated by W.S. Wilson) 1980. *Hagakure: The Book of the Samurai*. Tokyo/New York/San Francisco: Kodansha International, Ltd.

Sun Tzu. 1963. Translated by S. Griffith. *The Art of War*. Oxford: Oxford University Press.

Tappan, F. 1978. *Healing Massage Techniques*. Reston, VA: Reston Publishing Co., Inc.

Westbrook, A. and O. Ratti. 1970. *Aikido and the Dynamic Sphere: An Illustrated Introduction*. Rutland, VT: Charles E. Tuttle Company.

Williams, B., ed. 1975. *Martial Arts of the Orient*. London: The Hamlyn Publishing Group, Ltd.

Wilson, W., trans. 1982. *Ideals of the Samurai: Writings of Japanese Warriors*. Burbank, CA: Ohara Publications, Inc.

INDEX

Locators followed by *t* indicate tables.
Italicized page numbers indicate photos.

About the Authors

Doug Musser is a 23-year jujitsu practitioner who specializes in the Dan Zan Ryu style and holds the rank of 3rd-degree black belt. He currently manages and instructs at Illini Jujitsu—an Illinois-based dojo—and was a regional jujitsu director. In addition to jujitsu, he has practiced other martial arts, including Filipino Serrada Escrima, Chinese Wing Chun, and Northern Chinese Shaolin Kung Fu. He also practices massage therapy and is an instructor of traditional Japanese Restorative Massage. Musser lives in Champaign, Illinois.

Tom Lang has studied the martial arts for more than 25 years. He holds a 4th-degree black belt in Dan Zan Ryu jujitsu from the American Judo and Jujitsu Federation and a 2nd-degree black belt in Muso Shinden Ryu Iaido (Japanese sword drawing) from the All-Japan Kendo Federation. He also has trained in aikido, Filipino Kali, and police arts.

Sensei of the Kikushin Dojo at California State University, Chico, for several years, Lang has written several books and articles on the martial arts, including the *Kata Manual of the American Judo and Jujitsu Federation, An Introduction to Kodenkan Jujutsu, The Kyusho of Atemi, The History of the Tessen (Iron Fan), The Side-Handled Police Baton, The Japanese Short Staff,* and *Combat Techniques for the Cane and Three-Foot Stick.* Lang resides in Cleveland, Ohio.

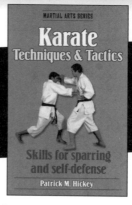
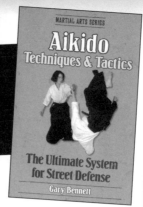